The Validation Plan

The
Validation
Plan

Awakening and Incorporating the
Essential Virtues for a Good Life Leading
to Respect, Harmony, and Peace

James E. Pirkle, PhD

iUniverse, Inc.
Bloomington

The Validation Plan

Awakening and Incorporating the Essential Virtues for a Good Life Leading to Respect, Harmony, and Peace

iUniverse books may be ordered through booksellers or by contacting:

iUniverse
1663 Liberty Drive
Bloomington, IN 47403
www.iuniverse.com
1-800-Authors (1-800-288-4677)

Because of the dynamic nature of the Internet, any web addresses or links contained in this book may have changed since publication and may no longer be valid. The views expressed in this work are solely those of the author and do not necessarily reflect the views of the publisher, and the publisher hereby disclaims any responsibility for them.

Any people depicted in stock imagery provided by Thinkstock are models, and such images are being used for illustrative purposes only.

Certain stock imagery © Thinkstock.

ISBN: 978-1-4759-7327-3 (sc)
ISBN: 978-1-4759-7328-0 (e)

Library of Congress Control Number: 2013902484

Printed in the United States of America

iUniverse rev. date: 2/26/2013

This book is dedicated to supportive family members, colleagues, and my wife, Joan, who has been a full partner in the Validation Program from the beginning.

Virtues do not arise in us by nature; we are not born with them. Even in the case of moral prodigies, each of us has to work in order to master the virtue or virtues of our choice. Once mastered, however, the virtue becomes a "second nature," a new power that habitually enhances our moral performance.

—John Bradshaw, *Reclaiming Virtue*, 45

We must accept that caring for children is the most vital concern any society has to address.

—Ibid., 94

The key to a happy, healthy relationship is … a person who validates your existing views and habits. The higher the quantity and quality of your relationships, the longer you live.

—Elizabeth Svoboda

A person can be really smart, but lack the social skills and emotional intelligence our world requires. Many people with killer scores on standardized tests go on to careers that leave them feeling less than satisfied, no matter how much money they earn. The Unabomber went to Harvard and taught math at Berkley, after all.

—Martha Brockenbrough, *Two Ways to Make a Kid Smarter*

Never doubt that a small group of thoughtful, committed citizens can change the world.

Indeed it is the only thing that ever has.

—Margaret Mead

Contents

Preface

Not unlike other teachers in other schools, we had a problem. Simply stated, in our day-to-day, side-by-side existence with students in an American school in the Netherlands, our students seemed frozen in their obsessively egocentric selves, insensitive toward others, with no "other-oriented" positive perspective at all. Instead, their focus in many situations leaned toward a negative perspective of others.

The first reflection of our concerns centered on the question, "What can we do about it now?" Daily, students interacted with one another in a social order that assured familiarity, yet there was an absence of spontaneous, positive comments/feedback or respect for one another. Their conversations were generally utilitarian or self-serving and too frequently were dominated by competitive or harsh interactions—something not new to teachers.

Our concern worked itself into a plan whereby youngsters would be placed in a program that would help find the good and positive in one another and give children the opportunity to reach out in respectful, caring, other-oriented ways. We sought to help them listen to one another more sincerely. We believed students could learn to openly understand and acknowledge one another in positive ways. It became an evolving plan of optimistic reinforcement, an eventual plan for positive human growth and kindness. We are still discovering its impacts. This plan is called the "Validation Program."

After working with the program for thirty-five years, it has grown and has had widespread significant positive impacts upon students' and adults' character development. We have found that the program has not only resulted in the positive character traits we were hoping for, but it also opened the doors for kindness to abound.

An important result has been the enhancement and enrichment of language arts skills. Students inherently grow in their vocabulary skills, automatically searching for appropriate words to describe their partners. Their writing is more motivated and precisely focused. They learn to read aloud and reread the validations they receive from their partners. They listen more closely to their classmates as they validate one another.

In fact, you will discover many more positive impacts upon our youth as you explore the book. As triple-time award winner of the Pulitzer Prize Edward Albee said whenever someone asked him to explain what his book or play was about, "If I had to explain it in one sentence, then the book would be just one sentence long."

It has been refreshing to continue to study, read, and provide workshops, presentations, and training sessions across the United States, Europe, Bermuda, Iceland, Newfoundland, and Norway. The program has also been presented at several annual conferences of a variety of professional education organizations.

May your journey through this information be cause for consideration of becoming an advocate and/or participant in the Validation Plan and Program.

Acknowledgments

Much appreciation is extended to the large numbers of teachers, educators, parents, and other organizations that have recognized and committed themselves to the program, witnessing firsthand the abundant positive outcomes for students and adults after implementing the program. Special recognition is extended to Gerry and Marg Schiele, who first shared with us the idea of "validation" more than thirty years ago. Many school administrators have also provided key support to teachers and students.

Specific recognition also goes to several colleagues who have been supporters and provided input toward the development of the program and this book: Ms. L. K. Mondrey; to all eleven hundred-plus sixth- through eighth-grade teachers, students, and administrators of Louisa County Middle School; Dr. Gerry Sokol; Ms. Michelle Wallace; Dr. MaryAnn Clark; the teachers, staff, students, and parents of Little Rissington K–8 school in England; Mr. Robert Bell; Dr. Rodman Webb; Del and Jane Frances; and Richard Cecil.

Introduction

If we are to reach real peace in this world ... we shall have to begin with the children.

—Mohandas Gandhi, Indian civil rights leader (1869–1948)

Boys and girls should be taught to think first of others; they should be infected with the wisdom to know that in making smooth the way of all lies the road to their own health and happiness.

—John Galsworthy, English novelist and playwright, Nobel Prize, 1932

This book is about a plan called the "Validation Program," which has been implemented for more than thirty-five years to awaken, infuse, and maximize the important virtues of life such as respect, cooperation, understanding, appreciation, and compassion toward others. The approach began in a small way and has substantially grown in many schools and organizations across many states, as well as abroad, since its inception in the mid-1970s.

There are a number of benefits, outcomes, and impacts that have occurred as a result of the program's influence. Students have developed appreciation, respect, and appreciation of one another unlike ever before. In a lively way, it establishes positive relations among students, the school, and its community. It also promotes thinking, writing, reading, speaking, and listening skills. As educator Ernest L. Boyer once said, "Language is the centerpiece of learning."

Moreover, youngsters become genuinely interested and engaged, owning the validation process and arriving home chatting about the program. When students are interested, engaged, and own the process, they are intrinsically motivated and more likely to learn the traits of good character, as well as the development of their intellectual skills. If we want students to rise to the level of expectations about their own character development and intellect, we can't do so without building support.

While it is important to know the definitions of the various virtues, acquiring these virtues is what the Validation Program builds—the essential virtues and character traits we all want to see in our schools, cities, states, and nations—the kinds of human beings we all long to see and to be—leading us to harmony, peace, and love.

This book is divided into two parts. Part 1 is titled "Why Implement the Validation Program?" This half of the book outlines the positive reasons for being connected to the validation concept and the program, as well as recognizing the numerous harms impacting us that can be diminished if we simply adopt the Validation Program throughout our schools and society. Part 2 of the book is titled "The Validation Program Implementation Plan" and is intended for teachers, administrators, other service organizations, and anyone else—even families—who decide, "Yep, I am going to give this a go!"

As an addendum to this introduction, you will find below some of the rather notable comments educators and students have shared about the impacts and success of the program over the years. These quotes are qualitative evidence of the impacts and success of the Validation Program. It is hoped many of these quotes will entice you and motivate you to learn about the program. After reading a few of these, you might later find it uplifting to read additional revealing testimonial letters and comments about the benefits and joys of the program, all of which can be found in Appendix H.

I received the following e-mail from a recently retired teacher, Robert Bell, in August 2012: "I was a UK-based teacher at AFCENT/AFNORTH International School in the Netherlands for twenty-six years. In the earlier part of my time there, we had an in-service day and you came to give a short course explaining the concept and practice of your 'validation' procedure. Little did I realize that course was to have a huge impact on my upper-elementary teaching for many years to come. I began 'validation' the following week and continued it, every week of every year, with my classes until I retired. This was in spite of wholesale changes and radical alterations in classroom curriculum and time-tabling. I would not—could not—drop 'validation' time. I valued above everything the strong, positive relationships that the weekly 'validation' time fostered. Indeed, I cannot think of another curriculum initiative that had an equal impact on my teaching during the course of my thirty-seven years of service."

From Sally Agee, eighth-grade science teacher, 2012: "Even though I had a particularly tough group this year in which to do validations, I do think the program is very much needed in all schools at this time in history when society teaches us to be so self-centered and cutthroat. Students must learn to consider others' feelings and the consequences of their actions on others! I believe the Validation Program can plant the seed to get this state of mind growing in our students."

From Rob Sarnoski, middle-school resource officer, 2012: "Validation is not just a program but a long-term investment in one's future. It enhances character development by helping individuals become more outwardly focused, to look beyond immediate surface characteristics (e.g., tall or short, thin or heavy, white or black, etc.) and see the good and true things about people. Validation implemented in the school setting, has the ability to create safer and more tolerant learning environments by reducing incidences of bullying, fighting, and other interpersonal conflict. Students embracing validation develop more positive attitudes while improving speaking, writing, and listening abilities, the skills essential to secondary and higher education. The actual investment in time and money to implement a Validation Program is minimal. From my experience, I can't imagine why any school system wouldn't make validation an integral part of their education program."

Another source highlighting the impacts of the Validation Program comes from some of the actual statements students have made about specific impacts the program has had upon them after their first experience with the program. These are actual word-for-word quotes. After reading the following comments from a variety of students, you may also see how an abundant number of other students would also benefit from the program. You will also find some students' comments embedded within the text of the book.

This weekly event is always a pleasure to work on. I've been looking at my classmates' work and skills closer and realize the kind of people they are. This might sound corny, but I have to admit the validation [experience] has taken some of the kids out from under their rock. I feel validation has helped out our class both mentally and physically, for each validation just seems to make you feel good all day.

—Twelfth-grade English honors student

This class has really come a long way. The students are much kinder now. I have particularly enjoyed this assignment. People need this more often all over the world and of all ages.

—Ninth-grade student

There's that "validation feeling." You feel your heart shudder, and a smile comes to your face as you read your validation to your validation partner. Or you could get that Validation feeling when you're having your validation read to you, or when you're reading it at home. You can't describe the validation feeling; you just have to experience it. Some people think it's for young. But no. Validations are for everyone.

—Twelfth-grade English honors student

It helps the people involved grow more self-confident and learn to accept others and to see their good qualities, many they never noticed before. Throughout the year, I realize there are many people I now consider good friends. But if it wasn't for the Validation Program, I would probably barely know them.

—Twelfth-grade student

◇◇◇◇◇◇◇◇◇◇◇◇◇◇◇◇◇◇◇◇◇◇◇◇◇◇◇◇◇◇ # PART 1
Why Implement the Validation Program?

Primary Reason #1:
Significant Character Benefits

Almost all the literature in the first 150 years or so focused on what could be called the character ethic as the foundation of success—things such as integrity, humility, fidelity, temperance, courage, justice, patience, industry, simplicity, modesty, and the Golden Rule.

—Stephen Covey, *The Seven Habits of Highly Effective People*

Character, in the long run, is the decisive factor in the life of an individual and of nations alike.

—Theodore Roosevelt (1858–1919)

Reason #1 is based upon the rationale of why it is critical to help youngsters develop an "other-oriented" perspective, positive relationships, and the essential virtues of life.

Now more than ever, it seems, is the time to implement and infuse the significant character benefits resulting from a program like Validation. Every day, newspapers and other media bombard us with horrid events and perplexing mishaps caused by those whose character is way off base. How long will we have the patience to bear the continual daily pain of atrocities and heartbreaks that make us scratch our heads and wonder, *What in the world is going on? Why is our nation filled with people who wreak havoc right and left across all cultures, neighborhoods, schools, offices, buildings, and even places of entertainment? What can we do that we instill in them the essential virtues to begin with that will turn them around to be the kind of positive, character-filled person who will not commit such atrocities?*

Whether we like to think about it or not, our nation's culture is much too awash with negativity, incivility, insults, bickering, bad-mouthing, harassment, self-centeredness, physical and mental abuses, violence, deaths, and hate groups. Yet there are few widespread commitments to do something about it all. Look at what our children learn when they are subjected to a world where our leaders, entertainment, and the press exude garbage bags full of vile and irresponsible rhetoric and behavior.

Little significant progress has occurred in terms of taking active, responsible, dedicated commitment to rectify such behaviors and thinking. Without grabbing the bull by the horns with a determined, dedicated, and sustained commitment to do what it takes to help us help others become good human beings and create a positive culture—inside and outside schools—we will not get there.

David Brooks, a prolific writer and accumulator of vast amounts of research relative to the world of character development and social behavior, has said, "We are good at teaching technical skills, but when it comes to the most important things, like character, we have almost nothing to say" (Brooks, 2012). We can't neglect an important part of students' well-being that integrates the "human goods" essential to any mentally and emotionally peaceful, responsible citizen. We can still get there if we have the conscious strength and courage to set the boat aright. We can help students develop habits to facilitate the moral character by emphasizing and having them engaged in a program like validation, which helps them learn and practice the virtues and behaviors we know are keys to success.

Over the years via the program, we've discovered our youngsters experienced a school environment where they began to feel and know they were valued at heart from all those they encountered. The adults and their classmates gave them genuine attention, understanding, and caring, absolute ingredients for wholesome development of themselves. An intuitive truth has emerged: without a warm, nurturing environment, students are less likely to learn. When students understand they are valued, respected, and appreciated for who they are, their levels of motivation and achievement become enhanced.

There is no doubt many families, churches, organizations, and clubs have a significant impact on the positive character development of our youth. And for that, many of us are especially thankful and appreciative.

By no means is there an implication that academic success and achievement is insignificant as a major mission of all schools. However, we have learned that students can excel academically, make all As, and still "flunk life." Competence without a strong moral conscience is failure personified. Emotional, social, and psychological intelligence cannot be shut in the closet or otherwise ignored.

The Character Education Partnership (CEP, 2010) organization has suggested there are two kinds of character: moral character and performance character. One's moral character relates to the virtues, values, and ethics in one's life: kindness, integrity, empathy, compassion, and so on. Performance character relates to the particular traits of one's personal effectiveness: self-responsibility, perseverance, stamina, determination, etc.

While it can be said they are two different components to character, both categories are valuable, overlap, and are incorporated within the domain of the Validation Program. Teachers who care about the character development of their students find that the Validation Program is a vehicle to help youngsters discover and learn about the various virtues within each character domain.

Additionally, we need to take advantage of as many opportunities as possible that might lead us to practical options for youngsters to work together positively. This program places them in a position where they "own" their own learning about character development. They become engaged in developing an other-oriented perspective. It puts each student in a role where they learn about and discover the good and true character traits of others—genuinely engaging them in learning, in discovering and adopting the critical virtues of life and sound character. Moreover, healthy positive connections and relationships between students grow and bring smiles to our faces.

> Let no one be deceived. The important things that happen in schools result from the interactions of personalities.
>
> —Willard Waller, American sociologist (1899–1945)

Let's start by addressing some of the topics, issues, and concerns related to why the Validation Program is an important program to consider.

It is always tempting to just jump into the description of any program. But before doing so, providing a rationale for any program or proposal is natural and important to many. If, however, you are already convinced that you would like to consider becoming involved in the program, and don't really want to read all the reasons why this program is needed, jump ahead to Part 2 of the book, "The Implementation Plan," written after years of learning what and how one might best go about putting the program into action. The manual applies to all grade levels, from kindergarten through high school, college, and beyond.

Primary Reason #2:
Our Suffocating Cultural Harms

When I first became involved with intercollegiate debate, the affirmative team had to identify the existing "harms" within the current system or society that stymied or impacted negatively upon any improvement needed. So, if we propose that our youngsters need assistance or support they are not getting to make them better students and character-filled human beings, we need to review the existing harms in our current system that identify why the current system has failed and could benefit from a program like Validation.

Several authoritative sources have identified significant concerns in our culture. The following are just some of the significant harms in our culture that negatively impact the moral/ethical character development of our youngsters, and even adults.

A. Bullying/Cyberbullying

We've all been bombarded with the persistent presence and onslaught of bullying over the past few decades. Bullying has been made worse via the availability and frequent use of the Internet to bully others--referred to as "cyberbullying." Few youngsters are exempt from face-to-face bullying or cyberbullying. A magazine article in *The Week*, "Battling Bullying," reports that more than half of fifteen- and sixteen-year-olds have been cyberbullied. The same article reports another study revealing that 60 percent of boys who were bullied in middle school had a criminal record by age twenty-four. Moreover, each year so many of our youth fear bullies so dreadfully that 160,000 become school dropouts (*The Week*, 2010).

Bullying is a significant harm that has been addressed by several school antibullying programs, the Olweus Bullying Prevention Program being one of the major programs. Other programs try to instill sensitivity, encouraging becoming more empathic and considerate of others. As the website www.stopbullyingnow.gov notes, "It takes the entire school community to create an inviting school where everyone feels they belong and are safe."

We have also learned that victims of ferocious bullying often become deeply alienated. They have fewer positive, authentic interactions, relationships, and friends. This kind of social isolation leads to a larger social fissure in our culture. We need to keep in mind that healthy relationships make for a healthy society.

The Validation Program can and has had turnaround results for those who are bullied and those who are bullies themselves. Students begin with the opportunity to become more "other-oriented," eventually overturning their self-centeredness and other negative behaviors. They are consistently informed and coached to become more other-oriented, focusing on the good traits of their classmates, and placed into the position of reinforcing the positive traits. Validation sends the message—consciously and unconsciously—that negativity is unacceptable. It is *not* what we are about. For most developing youths, sticks and stones may not break their bones, but ugly language and harassment too often hurt and break apart their stability.

In the past, we have heard how youth are dominated by genetics. Instead, their behavior is more likely the result of the norms of their neighborhood. We know the brain can form new neurons and create new neural pathways through life. When writing and reading validations to their partners, such mental stimulation helps create healthy social engagements. We can help turn youngsters around by placing them into a world of good company, members of which place them into an arena of learning about and incorporating the important virtues of life.

For further information about halting cyberbullying, you may want to visit this site: www.stopcyberbullying.org/parents/youth_empowered_solutions.html (Stop Cyberbullying, 2012).

B. Incivility, Negativity, and Cynicism

It seems negative thoughts and behaviors constantly surround us on news channels, in discussions, in movies, and on TV shows. They have worked their way into the norms of daily life. Vitriolic language or any other putrefied-tinged rhetoric cannot be justified. Negativity in any form—face-to-face bad-mouthing, biased thoughts, uncooperative attitudes toward others—have detrimental effects on our students and the climate of a school. It inherently disrupts the learning environment. Some believe civility is dead, oftentimes because there is little regard for the sheer respect, value, dignity, and significance of others.

How can we go about fostering positive relationships in life in a cultural arena of everyday incivility? We've learned good teaching is one foundation for creating and building relationships. Author Gary Smalley said, "Life is relationships; the rest is just details." Any organization, business, school system, etc. concentrates on developing positive relationships because it is essential for harmonious civility and success. Effective leaders learn this early on. Times change, but manners and civility should not.

Brooks reveals that British philosopher Phillip Blond has asserted that we "Look at the society we have become: we are a bipolar nation, a bureaucratic centralized state that presides over an increasingly fragmented, disempowered, and isolated citizenry" (Brooks, 2011).

Ironically, our political system is infected with rampant, rhetoric bullying dogma, especially during campaigns. If our students behaved publicly like our politicians behave publicly, would our school discipline policies ignore it as bullying? The messages our leaders are overtly sending is that it's okay to spew negativity right and left. Our politicians are so willing to vilify, berate, and belittle their opponents publicly and across the airways that we become bathed in bewilderment and animosity. Would our schools put up with this? Do our leaders think such constant criticism, negativity, and outright incivility is okay because "that's just the way it is in politics"? Do you think they realize polarization is taking place between us and them? Have they forgotten that sincere leaders are the major models of good character? Have they awakened to the fact that they are setting a tone for our youth and everyone to emulate? Yet at times the fate of our schools is often in the hands of our politicians. It often comes to mind what the results might be if our politicians were to formally and regularly validate one another.

C. Narcissism

The ancient story of Narcissus, who fell in love with his own reflection, became the foundation for the word *narcissism*—a pathological study of self-absorption, the sacred center of the universe—selfism.

Narcissism is prevalent throughout our society. Relative to our youth, Brooks reports, "In 1950, a personality test asked teenagers if they considered themselves an important person. Twelve percent said yes. By the late 1980s, 80 percent said yes" (191). He further elucidates that "we are all born with deep selfish drives—a drive to take what we can, to magnify our lusts. These drives warp perception" (Brooks, 2012).

Other narcissism-related words include *self-centered*, *ego-centered*, or *me-centeredness*. Narcissism is not only a deterrent to an emotionally and psychologically healthy person; it can be a harm to understanding and communicating with others as well. The ego is also bolstered by another anachronism. In the article referencing the ego by Scott Kaufman, "How to Spot a Narcissist," it was stated, "Reality TV breeds egoism because it's based on people overacting to matters of minor consequences" (Kaufman, 2011).

This sort of self-importance can negate an other-oriented perspective and empathy toward others. Youngsters who grow up with an oversized ego will be less likely to put others first. The obsession with oneself can be directly addressed in the classroom. The Validation Program basically provides the school and classroom an anti-narcissism mission and focuses on treating others respectfully, enhancing those connections that make a sense of community possible.

It can be fairly said that each of us has some bit of narcissism within us. However, the person who is especially high in self-esteem, vanity, grandiosity, entitlement, self-admiration, need for attention, and a classic braggart with all the right answers, is likely the one obsessed with narcissism. Whether we believe it or not, there are some in leadership positions who display clear evidence of narcissism. Yet it can also be said that when some of us are self-confident, self-assured, and self-sufficient, that does not mean we are excessive narcissists. It runs both ways. With the not-so-strictly narcissist, there is a balance.

Nelson Hultberg of Americans for a Free Republic (http://www.afr.org/) wrote, "Our society revels in an orgy of self-indulgence and self-abasement. The quest for moral reputation has been supplanted by an obsession for instant notoriety—a ferocious competition in attention-seeking. Reality TV lifts narcissists who flaunt their neuroses and intimacies before millions of video voyeurs."

D. Violence, Shootings, Homicides, and Suicides

Perhaps the most alarming harms occurring within our society, and among our youngsters, are those of violence, death, and other suicides. Canadian psychologist Frank Smith says the history of education can be summed up in seven words: "We learn from the company we keep."

If the primary company we keep is with those who are positive, kind, caring, and empathic, we learn these characterizes for ourselves. If we keep company with a lot of negatively predisposed, angry, bigoted, and hostile people, the same learning occurs.

Yet there are other "companies" we keep that have definitive negative impacts on us as well. How can we continue to be exposed to and keep company with the plethora of media so prevalent throughout our society and not be influenced? The widespread number of violent video games, movies, TV programs, and obscene materials (under the guise of "entertainment") are examples of some of the company we keep. Victims galore are killed or impaired by axes, guns, chainsaws, knives, dismemberment, being set on fire, or chopped into little pieces. And we rationalize that this is just "entertainment"? We dismiss it all. What hole will we crawl into next?

In a recent article "Violence 'Ages' Children's DNA" by Liz Szabo, a new study indicates that "violence has long-term scars on children's bodies, altering their DNA, causing changes that are equivalent to seven to ten years' of premature aging." She cites one study at the Duke Institute for Genome Sciences & Policy in NC, revealing "these kids could be expected to develop diseases of aging, such as heart attacks or memory loss, seven to ten years earlier than their peers" (Szabo, *USA Today,* 2012).

For various other examples and data showing the impacts of violence on us, you might want to explore the info in Appendix G. The website for the National Center of Educational Statistics provides specific data for each year. The information is massive and gut-wrenching. Here you will find one of the major sources showing actual data on the harms our youth and schools suffer. The horrid memories of Columbine, Virginia Tech, and Sandy Hook ES in Newtown, CT will remain with us forever.

Al Lewis's article, "Dead by 50? Thank You!" reports that the 378-page study by the Institute of Medicine and the National Research Council titled "U.S. Health in International Perspective: Shorter Lives, Poorer Health" has revealed that "Firearm homicides are 20 times higher in the U.S. than in the other wealthy countries" (Lewis, 2013).

We've heard many times that whenever a person commits a violent act, someone says, "Well, those people are just mentally ill, and there's just not much you can do about that." And the person is left alone. What we have learned is that we simply can't just assume some of our students are incapable of being helped. We can instead implement programs that might well positively impact the character development of many youngsters, even turning them around.

When psychologist Robert Fein was asked, "People often assume mass murderers must be mentally ill. Is that true?" he answered, "The great, great, great majority of people with mental illness never commit violent acts" (Marcus, 2010).

E. Corporal Punishment

This harm can be significant to many of our youngsters. Sometimes it is called paddling or spanking, and for many it may be considered a minor form of physical punishment or violence. Yet it still can cause complications. Many view this issue as an ineffective discipline method that has negative impacts on the mental and physical health of those who are its unfortunate recipients.

It can be said we humiliate children when we use corporal punishment. Some youngsters carry smoldering resentments into adulthood. The results of using physical prowess can teach children that violence is a way of solving problems, of expressing anger, of perpetuating aggression. Physical punishment is counterproductive.

Spanking is likely to teach children they can solve problems through aggression, preventing development of internal behavior controls. Sadly, in my opinion, I fear that spanking may well increase the probability of depression in an adult.

F. Focusing Primarily/Heavily on Academic Achievement

> Education worthy of its name is essentially education of character.
>
> —Martin Buber, philosopher (1878–1965)

Focusing on academic achievement in and of itself is not by any means one of the harms intended in the book. However, totally neglecting our students' character development because teachers and schools either do not want to focus on anything else except academic success, or are informed that it is not part of the school's responsibility to also focus on the moral and emotional intelligence of a child's character development, is an intentional or unintentional harm.

Many of us may wince when others suggest our educational system today is too overwhelmingly focused on academic achievement, intellectual knowledge, and passing standardized tests. Some teachers feel schools are diminishing the joy of life and learning by focusing solely on standardized tests, academics, and intellectual excellence tests, tests, and more tests. Several are frustrated our schools are not focusing seriously on helping develop our youngsters' character—believed to be a major (if not *the* major) key to success.

In an article titled "Social and Emotional Learning," Dr. Robin Stern quotes Dr. Maurice Elias, a leading child psychologist and researcher and expert on social and emotional learning (SEL) from Rutgers University. Dr. Elias explains the dangers of omitting social-emotional programs from our children's classrooms.

Many of the problems in our schools are the result of social and emotional malfunction and debilitation from which too many children have suffered and continue to bear the consequences. Children in class who are beset by an array of confused or hurtful feelings cannot and will not learn effectively. In the process of civilizing and humanizing our children, the missing piece is, without doubt, social and emotional learning. Protestations that this must be outside of and separate from traditional schooling are misinformed, harmful, and may doom us to continued frustration in our academic mission and the need for Herculean efforts in behavioral damage control and repair. The roster of social casualties will grow ever larger. (Stern, 2012)

It is a no-brainer that without the development of good character, we will seldom succeed in many arenas of life. How many tyrants and dictators, murders and sex abusers, swindlers and drug dealers are successes? Experience has informed us that not one parent has ever complained about schools helping students develop good behavior and becoming responsible citizens who support the virtues of fairness, compassion, cooperation, helpfulness, courtesy, punctuality, integrity, justice, patience, modesty, and many of the other virtues as well.

David Brooks, exceptionally versed in the domain of sociology, further underlines the need for education to take on the cause of character development: "Modern society has created a giant apparatus for the cultivation of the hard skills, while failing to develop the moral and emotional faculties down below. Children are coached on how to jump through a thousand scholastic hoops. We are good at talking about material incentives, but bad about talking about emotions and intuitions. We are good at teaching technical skills, but when it comes to the most important things, like character, we have almost nothing to say" (Brooks, 2011).

Consequently, it is incumbent upon us to formulate a plan for developing these values in our students. We need to be committed to facilitating such a movement, especially to help teachers create opportunities for getting students to understand and respect others and to become responsible citizens of character. Moreover, we have learned our youngsters require a sacrifice and a strong, honest commitment to more than just academic success. Do we have the determination to work together to do so?

G. Harsh Role of Competition

Competition reigns far too supremely throughout our culture. It becomes a major focus for many of our citizens. It is fun, engaging, and motivational yet becomes obsessive to many of us. It dominates our attention and focus. Unfortunately, competitiveness creeps into some of our noncompetitive school activities. Competition with one's classmates as a major motivation for learning needs to be critically assessed. Competition can cause students to think everyone else can be an obstacle to their own success. If we don't put competition into proper balance in youngsters' lives, they will continue to fall into the pit of its consumption. Their conscience will focus less and less on the critical virtues important to their success.

H. Dropouts

The reality of dropouts from America's school system is gripping and disturbing. The total number of high-school dropouts *each day* equals 8,300, a total of 3,030,000 a year. Plus, 36 percent of all dropouts happen in the ninth grade, and 75 percent of US crimes are committed by a high-school dropout (Statistics Brain, 2012).

A key to keeping students in school is to engage them directly in their entire school experience. Too many dropouts became more and more disenchanted with schooling because they were not personally engaged or connected with their school, others in the school, or school activities, clubs, or organizations. The Alliance for Excellent Education organization reports, "Nationwide, about seven thousand students drop out every school day. Research shows that a lack of student engagement is predictive of dropping out" even though they may be doing well academically and despite whatever their background may be (Alliance for Excellent Education, 2010). A program like Validation specifically engages and reinforces each student while supporting the development of the whole child, thus increasing the likeliness for keeping students in school.

I.   "iCrazy" Technology

In a recent *Time* magazine article titled "iCrazy Technology," Tony Dokoupil clearly specifies that emerging research underlines the pervasive "incarnation" of the Internet. It is not only making us "dumber or lonelier, but more depressed and anxious, prone to obsessive-compulsive and attention-deficit disorders, even outright psychotic. Normal people are breaking down in sad and seemingly new ways." This article also reports a 1998 study by Carnegie Mellon University revealing that web use over two years resulted in blue moods, loneliness, and the loss of real-world friends (Dokoupil, 2012). What we've also learned from youngsters who experience the Validation Program is that their moodiness and loneliness is diminished and they feel valued, respected, and connected with others.

Our youngsters today are too frequently removed and isolated from what used to be everyday face-to-face connections. Strong relationships are less likely to be cemented via remote visual language. Dokoupil points out that the impact of the Internet and mobile technology causes significant problems, including the dissolution of social skills and healthy relationship building. He also reports a study that has shown the brains of Internet addicts look like the brains of drug and alcohol addicts. Numerous neuroscience studies have shown that the brain rewires itself in many ways—and across many age groups.

Obsession with the technology domain is clear. Dokoupil notes that teens spend some seven hours in an average day with tech devices. Plus, they process 3,700 texts a month. One-third glue their eyes to their devices before they even get out of bed. What kind of world is this creating? We now know that the Diagnostic and Statistical Manual of Mental Disorders (DSM-V) has defined this obsession as an "Internet Addiction Disorder."

Dokoupil provides more evidence and gripping harms of the influence of technology. One young couple became so engrossed watching a virtual baby show on a website that their own infant died. A young fellow bludgeoned his mother for suggesting he get off the Internet. And so far, at least ten "ultra-Web users" sat so long they died from blood clots. Dokoupil also reports that a high-school student, presumably because he spent an overly extensive twenty-four hours on his iPhone, wound up in an asylum.

Sharon Jackson notes, "Ever-present tech devices can push our crazy buttons and has made us a little lazier in keeping up and working on strong relationships." Moreover, she reveals that research psychologist and computer educator Larry Rosen of California State University has found that "technology is causing some people to exhibit symptoms of problems including narcissistic personality disorder, obsessive-compulsive disorder, addiction and depression, among others" (Jackson, 2012).

Is enough enough?

Not to acquiesce to this harm, but technology itself is not singularly the primary fault of incivility or obsessiveness. But it does throw open the door to hide behind and blast away! We are responsible for our own lives, but we have too few "balance guidance" mechanisms or firm realizations to keep us from going overboard and instilling the compulsive habits of technology. The impacts of Facebook, Twitter, YouTube, et al., offer the irresistible opportunity for many to grow a huge ego, since they can increase their fame.

J. Letting Loners Linger

The deepest despair is not being willing to be oneself. If your essential core is denied, you get sick. Even if denied, your core persists and presses underground for development and makes you despise yourself until acknowledgement is given.

—Peter Koestenbaum, philosopher

It is fair to say all teachers have had to deal with at least one or more "loners" in their classrooms. Something has gone awry with these youngsters. Often they are troubled, exhibit traits out of the ordinary, are typically quiet, and appear "disconnected."

Some youngsters do not necessarily see themselves as "loners." The may just be sad or don't feel like they are part of the group (or groups) of kids they are with. Unfortunately, sometimes they are just plain left alone, for a variety of reasons. Some see themselves as misfits and easily slide into social isolation. Some begin to lash out in bizarre ways. Some become angry. Some look for others like themselves. Some become members of gangs. Loners tend to have more negative thoughts and negative interactions with others.

Some youngsters are just shy, but they still need understanding, support, and help. If we can reach just one loner, or shy student, and help him or her break out of his or her shy world, it's worth the effort. It is never too early or two late to make a difference in our youngster's lives. The earlier the intervention, the better. But we have found that it is never too late for middle and high school students to be positively impacted.

Many of these youngsters have been turned around as a result of the Validation Program and become valued members of the classroom and society. We might not only help one loner or shy person break out of her or his isolation, we might diminish the likelihood of multiple atrocities he or she might inflict upon others later on down the road.

Educator Charles Haynes firmly believes "Developing students' hearts is what educators are called to do. Each and every small act of honesty, service, responsibility, and compassion that teachers and administrators encourage daily in their students—and model consistently in their own lives—helps create moral and civic habits of the heart that instill in students the courage to care" (Haynes, 2009). In Haynes's opinion (not intentionally negating academic achievement), "Education's highest aim is to create moral and civic habits of the heart. Schools should be the laboratories for acts of conscience."

Haynes refers to the essential virtues as "habits of the heart." But these habits are not created instantaneously and do not grow overnight. It takes time, perseverance, and a genuine commitment from us as significant others, parents and teachers, to help embed these "habits of the heart." We are the ones to help build their consciences, to do what is right, to treat all fairly and with compassion.

Haynes believes "many of our schools are prohibiting students from practicing civic habits of the heart," and that "growing numbers of schools are shutting down student voice and avoiding discussion of ethical issues."

When we commit ourselves to help students learn the principles and virtues necessary to civil life, we will see the emergence of a wholesome culture focusing on the common good, on harmony, compassionate connectedness, and peace.

When the Validation Program is sincerely implemented with commitment, with every student actively engaged in looking, seeing, understanding, valuing, and respecting others, then we will help them build habits of heart and conscience critical to our existence.

An article in *The Week* magazine, "Creating a 'Mind Meld' by Talking," illustrates that genuinely connecting with others in a sincere setting (the purpose of which is to communicate with each other positively) is not always easy or automatic. But when Validation partners share their positive points about one another, the article underscores that "they often feel as if they've just 'clicked.' A new study of that phenomenon has found that conversing can produce an almost eerie synchronization of brainwaves, so that the speaker and listener experience a kind of 'mind meld'" (*The Week*, 2010).

Key Related Components of Validation

A. The Role of Leadership

> In the arena of human life, the honors and rewards fall to those who show their good qualities in action.
>
> —Aristotle

All professional educators are leaders. Whether a teacher, an administrator, or an educational specialist, we are all leaders. The responsibilities may be different, but each of us automatically resides in the arena of leadership.

In schools, administrators may be the first ones who come to mind as "educational leaders," such as superintendents, assistant superintendents, and central office professional educators, principals, assistant principals. When it comes to students, the most significant leader of all is their classroom teacher.

Larger positive impacts of the Validation Program occur when the program is implemented school-wide in all teachers' classrooms. Consequently, it is essential that school administrators are clearly up front, committed leaders of the program. Without the administrators' sincere leadership, support, commitment, and belief in the program, its success is likely to be compromised. A critical aspect of effective leaders is that they significantly impact others by modeling a value-based leadership style, the virtues promoted in the Validation Program.

Administrators' leadership, support, and commitment to the program are important to teachers. Teachers must know the administrators totally support them during their implementation of the program.

After years of studying and being in the role of educational leadership, we've learned the least successful leaders are those who are rather autocratic, authoritative, self-serving, unethical, untrustworthy, or narcissistically "me-centered." We have also learned that especially effective leaders are other-oriented. They are cast into the role of being what has been called in many institutions "serving leaders." This role has also been referred to as "servant leaders." But some people may semantically have a negative perception or response to the word "servant."

> I don't know what your destiny will be, but one thing I do know: the only ones among you who will be really happy are those who have sought and found how to serve.
>
> —Albert Schweitzer

The typical hierarchical pyramid of an organization has to be turned upside down in the school setting. The administration is not at the top. The people closest their constituencies (students and parents) are at the top of the pyramid. Realizing we are there to serve others foremost, step back and reflect on what educational leadership is all about. We learn to put our ego out of the way. If leaders don't put others for whom they work first, then two of the key characteristics of successful leadership—humility and trust—will likely fall by the wayside and diminish our success of working together as a team.

Another key component is to possess humility. Without humility we will limit our progress and success as a leader. Only by doing so will we create the kind of relationships that define our virtues.

Charles Stillwell, headmaster of St. Christopher's school in Richmond, Virginia, asks all of us to rally "behind a crucial common goal: the importance of developing in our young people the character, wisdom, and skills necessary for ethical leadership" (Stillwell, 2011).

B. Validation's Connection to Development of Moral Intelligence

Always do the right thing. This will gratify some people and astonish others.

—Mark Twain

The Validation Program is an example of the burgeoning "positive psychology" movement as endorsed by the American Psychological Association. In 1997, Robert Coles wrote *The Moral Intelligence of Children*, an ideal information source for all who work with youngsters. He defines and delineates the concepts of "goodness" and the development of "the Good Person" (Coles, 1997).

Our experiences with validation have revealed that some youngsters already have a certain moral indifference toward others, and some also have a built-in disregard for others, all with no justification. Validation is a method that can alert us to the failure or success of our moral intelligence and can be enhanced when our students are given the chance to learn about the virtues that lead to moral intelligence, and then adopt the moral habits and virtues they see in others. They want to be the good youngsters they see in others.

Another arena related to moral intelligence is "emotional intelligence." Daniel Goleman coined this term in reference to how we handle our own emotions and feelings; how well we empathize with others, and how we learn to cope and develop our emotional lives (Goleman, 1995).

So is there a balance between emotional intelligence and cognitive intelligence? David Brooks notes, "Work by David Van Rooy suggests no more than 5 percent of a person's emotional perceptiveness can be explained by the sort of overall cognitive intelligence we track with an IQ score" (Brooks, 2011).

Furthermore, Bradshaw hits the nail on the head: "Our critical role in naming, mirroring, and validating the child's affects is the way to develop a child's emotional intelligence" (Bradshaw, 2009).

Schools have always had a mission of socializing our students as we prepare them for life ahead. Students need essential nurturing to develop the moral habits of responsibility, integrity, manners, perseverance, etc., in order to successfully complete their work and become productive class members. Hence, they learn the moral rules of life necessary for a society to function well.

C. The Roles of Neuroscience and Nature versus Nurture

Even the tiniest shift of focus toward the positive or the negative can tilt myriad brain circuits, strengthening or weakening connections and circuits within our rainy brain or our sunny brain.

—Merel van Beeren

We often hear people talking about nature versus nurture as an explanation of who and what we are. Sometimes it suggests these two philosophies have been in perpetual conflict. While both views have merit, they also complement each other. Simply put, "nature" is associated with heredity and "nurture" is associated with environmental impacts.

Genetically determined connections do form innate templates in the architecture of the brain. However, the experiences we face in life also have impacts on reshaping the mind and bringing about patterns of new behavior. In discussing the role of neuroscience on this issue, my nephew, John Campbell, a PhD in neuroscience currently at Harvard University, has verified that biologists, psychologists, and neuroscientists have learned from a growing body of research that the brain is not a fixed entity or hardwired. Neuroscience research has revealed that the brain has "plasticity" or "neuroplasticity," meaning the brain has the ability to reorganize itself by forming new neural connections throughout life and can reprogram itself. For example, many of our brains are quickly becoming programmed to be Internet- and tech-dominant and may result in shortchanging the literate side of the brain.

John Bradshaw notes, "It is human connections that shape the neural connections from which our mind emerges" (Bradshaw, 2009).

The neuroplasticity of the brain illustrates that we can and do change. We're not just "locked" into previous or old patterns of thought or behavior.

We've learned that the Validation Program, over time, promotes youngsters to probe more deeply and discover the suitable descriptors, principles, and vocabulary defining the virtues, characteristics, and principles that lie within us. The Validation Program gives the brain a pathway of opportunities for literary digging and discovering the notable attributes of humanity and consciousness that define the best of human beings. The human connections that occur in the program build those neural connections, leading to positive and healthy relationships we all want to see for everyone. All teachers, therefore, are "nurture-ologists" in helping students along this path.

D. Listening

There are ample opportunities to help our students develop positive listening habits. The Validation Program offers one of those opportunities. In addition, teachers can stress the importance of listening closely and thoughtfully to others. Whenever students listen closely to one another, the brain processes the positive language being used and the effects of positive communication with one's partner are enhanced.

The Validation Program gives students an open door to focus on the listening component of this language arts skill—sometimes the least language arts skill youngsters learn about. One approach we can share with our students is to introduce them to Dr. Ralph Nichols, who wrote an article on "Listening to People" (Nichols, 1957–99). While at the University of Minnesota, he wrote an illuminating speech on "The Art of Listening" and is, without a doubt, the most oft-quoted expert in the field of listening. He was a founding and lifetime member of the International Listening Association.

In "Listening Is a Ten-Part Skill," he outlines the "Ten Worst Listening Habits of the American People." Many of these bad listening habits, and their consequential good listening habits, can be taught. You may want to listen to his speech and perhaps have students listen as well. It can be heard at the following website: http://www.listen.org/Nichols10Partspeech.

You might also find the following websites helpful to you and your students in terms of learning more about listening skills and habits (both good and bad). Visit the International Listening Leadership Institute (http://listeningleaders.com/home.html) and the International Listening Association (http://www.listen.org/) websites.

An additional thought to keep in mind about listening comes from Stephen Covey's *The Seven Habits of Highly Effective People*. Habit number five states, "Seek first to understand [and] then to be understood."

E. Critical "Other-Oriented" Perspective

All children need a sense of connectedness to a community, engagement in something beyond self, and an inner compass to help them resist negative cultural and street lures.

—Marian Wright Edelman, founder and president, Children's Defense Fund

Many of the harms addressed earlier give us sensible reasons for becoming more other-oriented. The primary approach when beginning the program is its focus on becoming more other-oriented. To help youngsters begin to find the constructive good in others, placing them into the active role of being able to truly focus on one another helps them begin to have positive relationships and an honest interest in others, and builds trust and caring among one another. Figuratively, the Validation Program provides each youngster a telescope and a microscope as tools toward becoming other-oriented.

Otherwise, if we continue to support the notion that it is okay to categorize others in a negative way, stereotyping, biases, prejudices, discriminations, and intolerance become part of one's persona.

There are numerous ways of approaching and stressing the importance of developing an other-oriented perspective. Before we start, ask yourself how many people give you the impression they are truly other-oriented. How about yourself? Would others say you are definitely, somewhat, or not at all an other-oriented person?

Do other people genuinely focus on you during conversations? Do they sincerely listen to you, seldom interrupt, and look directly at you? Do they do most of the talking? Do they ever ask you many questions that give you evidence they are indeed interested in you? Do they show genuine empathy when the conversation touches on sensitive issues?

People easily pick up on whether you show any sincere interest in them (and vice versa), and whether or not you show the slightest hint that you care. When others learn you really aren't very other-oriented and show no sense of caring about others, it becomes a blight on your reputation and character.

As we look around at others around us, how many would you say appear to be so busy with themselves and their lives that all they seem to talk about is themselves?

As youngsters develop, how many opportunities provide them with real-life chances to focus on others, to look for and consciously become aware of the good in others? Unless children, students, and even adults find themselves immersed in opportunities that are structured to give them the chance to focus directly on others, becoming an other-oriented person is consequently problematic.

We have all learned that if we want students to truly own the responsibility for whatever they study and learn, they will do so best if they are directly in charge of the learning experience. Sure, we can hope they will learn by lecture, by watching videos or films, reading how-to articles or books, and many other approaches to learning. But if you are directly in charge, it's yours 100 percent, and motivation to learn is inherent.

Learning about infusing character traits, virtues, and positive behavior cannot be taught in a single thirty-minute lesson. The sustained reinforcement needed to do so is not done in a week or a month either. Such reinforcement needs to begin early in schools and stressed throughout the year.

Then how do we go about doing so? The Implementation Plan, in the latter part of this book, explains how. Changing the approach to a school's disciplinary, communications, and interactions framework is easier for some than others. But what is crucial to success is the genuine buy-in of the teachers and administrators.

Everyone loves other-oriented people because they put less attention on themselves and they listen. To realize the benefits of becoming an other-oriented person, consider the occurring results. The other-oriented person automatically finds himself or herself seeking to understand others, making him or her a better communicator as a result. When understanding does occur, the other-oriented person becomes much more likely to appreciate and respect the person. These benefits don't necessarily occur in a singular, linear progression. They occur in a holistic fashion, leading one to become a caring person possessing one of the significant human virtues: empathy.

At the end of one recent school year, an eighth-grade Louisa County, Virginia, middle-school teacher who had implemented the Validation Program wrote, "The Validation Program created a paradigm shift in the attitudes that influenced relationships between students; students and teachers; and students, teachers, staff, and administration. It made our classes and our school a much more friendly, encouraging, caring, and emotionally safe place."

F. The Empathy Component

Many scientists believe the ability to unconsciously share another's pain is a building block of empathy, and through that emotion, morality.

—David Brooks, 2011

Empathy (from the Greek word *pathos*) is one of the virtues that an other-oriented person is likely to pick up along the way. She or he is by far more likely to garner a host of understandings of the other virtues of life by watching, listening, and focusing on the virtues of those surrounding her or him. Empathy is crucial to a healthy, caring, and well-adjusted personality, as well as to a healthy society. Consider painting a picture for students illustrating that too many people today live in the "me generation," rather than the "we generation."

Clifford Nass, a communications professor at Stanford, told the *New York Times* that our heavy dependence on technology diminishes empathy by limiting how much people truly engage with one another. "The way we become more human is paying attention to each other," he says. "It shows how much you care" (Nass, 2010).

Validation opens the door to understanding others, to recognizing and sharing the feelings of others. And, bingo, out pops the virtue of caring, the core of empathy. As we learn to walk in another person's shoes, doing so nurtures our relationships with others. Creating safe, secure, kind, and caring relationships and environments provides the nutrients for the growth of empathy. A warm, nurturing environment is the apex of positive development. And teachers are a major model for students, although I have heard some teachers tell their students something to the effect of, "I am not here to be liked." Is this a rationalization of their incapability or downright stubborn-headedness to be a truly empathic person?

The organization SCAN (Stop Child Abuse Now) notes that children can be taught the beginnings of empathy early. It suggests we continue to challenge children to think of others by giving them opportunities to experience others' lifestyles (SCAN, 2011). Our job is to help our students walk in each other's shoes, even those they don't know, don't like, or don't resemble. Validation helps them do just that.

Many teachers know helping develop students' hearts and minds is our job and is what we are "called" to do. And if we don't personally know we are "called" to be a teacher, helping students learn such character traits as empathy, we need to bow out of the profession a.s.a.p.

You may want to review Appendix J for additional informative empathy-tools websites.

G. The Climate and Culture of Your Classroom and School

> If we've learned anything from research into the characteristics of effective schools, it's that they possess team spirit, a real sense of purpose.
>
> —Chester Finn, Vanderbilt University

All classrooms and schools have their own particular climate and culture. "Climate" is often associated with words used to describe or characterize the "atmosphere" within the group, class, school, business, etc. It is also defined by how people feel about their school. Climate can be said to be either on the positive or negative side, or somewhere in between. When the climate is good, people typically enjoy coming to school.

"Culture" usually refers to the cognitive description, or perceived explanation, of what the classroom or school believes and exhibits in terms of its major goals, vision, and mission. A school often spells out its culture in its mission statement. Whether or not that mission statement is actualized is proof—or not—about its culture.

Climate and culture overlap. They are independent in definition but bonded in outcomes.

The classroom or school could be described as uplifting, energetic, happy, or somber. Some can be described as independent sanctuaries—serene and secure, or disorganized and hectic. Some are defined by autocratic dictators; some are defined as a cooperative participatory democracy. Some schools have evidence that their mission has been accomplished. Some do not have the evidence. Some have fulfilled their specific goals; some have not.

What we have found is that school climate and attachment to others are keys to stability, harmony, and positivism within the school. We have also learned that failed connections between students and faculty can lead to a shattered and disconnected school climate. When we know such disconnects do occur we can intervene.

Validation has had success in positively affecting the classrooms' and schools' climate and culture. Teachers and administrators have reported a noticeable change toward the acquisition of those positive character traits, norms, beliefs, and behaviors that we all hope to see in classrooms and schools. Faculty, administrators, personnel, and students meld into a kind of organic unit that begins to think in terms of "we" rather than "me." There is a student and adult realization of respect, cooperation, and continuous growth.

> The nature of the relationships among the adults who inhabit a school has more to do with the school's quality and character, and with the accomplishment of its pupils, than any other factor.
>
> —Roland Barth, founder, The Principals' Center at
> Harvard Graduate School of Education

When teachers and administrators genuinely commit as a collaborative team to the mission of the Validation Program and continue to support one another, positive and sincere outcomes regularly occur among students and educators affecting the climate and culture of the school and classrooms. Everyone begins to develop, to witness, and to embrace the beliefs they never consciously knew or understood before. They enter the domain of being more other-oriented. If resolving conflicts is really important to us, we can only get there by taking a backseat to the "stuckness" of our own egoistic perspectives and by considering that others' perspectives may be valid after all. The importance of nurturing a school climate conducive to mutual respect and dignity is identified in Standard 2 for school leaders of the Interstate School Leaders Licensure Consortium (Educational Leadership SuperSite, 1996).

Issues/Concerns to Keep in Mind

A. The Various "Self" Issues

By reading some of the comments students have written about the results of the program for them, there is no doubt it has enhanced their self-esteem. Abraham H. Maslow's (1908–70) "Hierarchy of Needs" explains human behavior in terms of basic requirements for survival and growth. These requirements, or needs, are arranged according to their importance and their power to motivate the individual. The basic physical requirements, such as food, water, or oxygen, constitute the lowest level of the needs hierarchy. These needs must be satisfied before other, higher needs become important to individuals. Needs at the higher levels of the hierarchy are less oriented toward physical survival and more toward psychological well-being and growth.

His fourth level of needs, "esteem," specifies we all need a fairly healthy degree of confidence and self-esteem. As our needs are met, we are strengthened and motivated to move forward toward greater levels of accomplishment and well-being. Eventually, we may reach the highest scale, "self-actualization," realizing our full potential. At this level, one is likely to be rather secure and capable of focusing on doing what he or she is meant to do in life, developing his or her talents and abilities to their fullest extent.

There are a variety of ways people have defined self-esteem over the years. Some equate self-esteem with self-worth. Some constructs include self-concept as a component of self-esteem, and there are overlaps with all these. But for brevity's sake, it seems most perceive the concept of self-esteem as generally relating to how one emotionally "feels" about oneself. One may feel "good" about himself or herself for a variety of reasons. However, we can over-focus on building one's self-esteem to the point of oversaturation, which leads to an inflated ego and self-centeredness. Sometimes praising students will give them a "big head," and they consequently will likely seek continued praise because they want to please the teacher. This can cause unjustifiably inflated self-esteem. Some have thought that if we can get students to strictly feel good about themselves, they will become good people. Feeling good about oneself does not equal behaving in an ethical manner. Pumping up one's self-esteem is not the primary focus of the Validation Program.

In Harriet Brown's recent article, "The Boom and Bust Ego," she notes, "Self-esteem, as a concept, has had wild ups and downs since the '70s. The newest take is that the less you think about your own self-esteem, the healthier you will be." In the same article she also cites research which "found no evidence that high self-esteem made people better students, more successful at work, or healthier" (Brown, 2012).

Self-esteem has also been construed as being a rather simplistic way of explaining one's success and overall feelings about oneself. However, there is a difference between how one "feels" (good or bad) and what he or she has just done. When our achievements are based on hard work, we may feel good about it. But that is not what it is all about. What is more important is to help youngsters develop a solid and true *self-concept*. Our self-concept is affiliated with the reality and recognition that we have certain amounts of knowledge, abilities, skills, etc. Am I good at math? History? Do I have good spatial skills in reading a map and know precisely where to go? Can I walk a balance beam with ease? We may feel good about doing so, but that's different from what is happening and what we can actually "do," which is building one's self-concept.

Equally important is *self-worth*. Our self-worth is kindled by knowing we are valued and appreciated for what we can honestly do well. If I am good at math and know for sure I am, and I know others value me for that particular ability or skill, then my self-worth is sound, and I am rationally comfortable and secure with myself on this domain.

We do not want validation to be primarily about puffing up youngsters. We do want to help reinforce and build their self-concept and self-worth. But there are other more important outcomes we seek. Development of the essential virtues and positive relationships leading to trust, understanding, and appreciation of others, and building the roads to harmony, unity, and peace are much more important.

One last concept is called *self-efficacy*. The typical definition of this is a person's belief about his or her ability and capacity to accomplish a task or to deal with the challenges of life—the measure of one's own competence to complete tasks and reach goals. This concept is also closely tied to one's "internal locus of control." If we have an "external locus of control," we attribute our success to external factors outside our control, such as luck or chance. Students who have an internal locus of control have a rather secure self-confidence. They realize their own abilities, not some outlying force or random factor, determine their success. Students who have a substantial internal locus of control perform better, can see beyond themselves, and realize they can adjust, change, see anew, and take control of their own destiny. They are capable of asking themselves, "Do I understand these various virtues of character?" "Can I comprehend what I am hearing?" "Can I picture and associate with the dilemmas and/or the positive things I see in others?" By identifying, valuing, and incorporating the virtues and values into their own lives, their sense of self-efficacy blossoms.

Teachers implementing the Validation Program learn that students begin to develop ownership and responsibility for finding and conceptualizing the good in others. Because validation is enmeshed in a classroom culture where everyone's "self" is positively engaged, it also serves as a sort of collective subliminal peer pressure that affects other students, building on the importance of possessing the virtues they see in one another. The validation construct reflects and is embedded within all the above "self" identifiers. The program has a positive, personal-character-development impact on each of the domains of self. The program lies within the affective and cognitive domains of self-development. If we don't help meet the needs of students for their various selves, they will not be interested in acquiring the knowledge and skills essential to their own futures.

B. The Praise Paradox

Focusing on the semantics of words and spending some time reflecting on the various meanings of words is automatically part of the teaching, reading, writing, speaking, and listening world. We are aware of the word *vocabulary* as we walk the aisles of the classroom. Much concentration on the study of vocabulary is on the *denotative* (dictionary) meanings of words. Some time is also spent on the *connotative* (emotional associations of words and the feelings and images they conjure) meanings of words.

One such word is *praise*, a word to be tiptoed around. If we think the word *praise* is just another word for *feedback*, we need to be careful. Too often the purpose of praise turns out to be a matter of benefiting the giver rather than the recipient. And too often students will continue whatever they do for "teacher-pleasing" reasons.

This is one of the reasons we use the words *acknowledging* or *recognizing* students rather than the emotional affiliation that praise connotes. Sure, we may want to enhance students' performance, promote the right or acceptable kinds of behavior, or help them feel good about themselves. But in the way *praise* is sometimes comprehended, it can fail to achieve these objectives.

We have all heard adults use highly sweetened baby-talk vocal tones as they talk to young children. Subliminally they are saying to themselves something like, "You are so great about what you just did that I want you to continue doing it forever to be sure you please me." These kinds of vocal "sweet" inflections may very well lead to the opposite of what is really intended. And such approaches can be a deterrent to the development of one's internal locus of control.

Rather than *praise*, we use the words *acknowledgment* or *recognizing* whenever we talk about the good qualities we find in others. We are not trying to boost their egos. We are professionally and rather matter-of-factly using ordinary conversational objective vocal tones to reinforce the efforts they make. The main focus for us to acknowledge or recognize students is to do so based on their efforts. We fear their motivation may actually diminish since they are simply being sugar-coated.

We have learned to be careful of bestowing extrinsic rewards upon students for fear of entering that domain of enabling and indulging students.

Effective teachers learn what kinds of feedback are relevant, effective, or ineffective. Sharpening our feedback skills is one of teachers' most effective tools. You might find Marge Scherer's article, "Finessing Feedback" and accompanying video of special interest on this tropic (Sherer, 2012).

Another helpful and refreshing source on this issue is Jenny Edwards's little book *Inviting Students to Learn: 100 Tips for Talking Effectively with Your Students* (Edwards, 2010).

The Validation Program is focused on acknowledging or recognizing students' self-awareness and self-determination in order for them to continue embracing the virtues of life and enhancing their own intrinsic motivation to become a good quality human being and responsible citizen. We encourage students to be as specific as they can when validating their partners, to steer away from phony comments and competition. Moreover, our intention is to communicate warmth, respect, concern, encouragement, and support, leading to unconditional appreciation, acceptance, and caring about one another. This intention is not in the connotative domain of *praise*.

C. Does Validation Only Happen in School?

While the program was initially infused into schools—and still is the main location where validation takes place—it has also worked its way into organizations, families, faculty, superintendents' meetings, and in personal interactions with others. We've learned the entire school community can start on the path toward ensuring our schools create a positive environment where all students feel valued, worthy, safe, cooperative, respectful, etc.

D. Utilize the Various Virtues Supporting and Enhancing the Program

Several sources have identified and elaborated on the specific virtues teachers can use to assist them and their students to become familiar with and learn about the various virtues. You may wish to access several of the following websites, all about the various virtues:

http://www.virtuescience.com/virtuelist.html\
http://en.wikipedia.org/wiki/List_of_virtues
http:// www.worldlanguageprocess.org/comic%20books/virtues%20list.htm
http:// www.wisdomcommons.org/virtues.

This ends Part 1. While you may well wonder why other harms, suggestions, items to consider, etc. are not included, hopefully this part of the book has provided you sufficient cause to consider implementing the Validation Program.

Enter Part 2.

◇◇◇◇◇◇◇◇◇◇◇◇◇◇◇◇◇◇◇◇ # PART 2
The Validation Program Implementation Plan

The Validation Idea Begins

To educate a person in mind and not in morals is to educate a menace to society.

—Theodore Roosevelt (1858–1919)

Most people say that it is the intellect which makes a great scientist. They are wrong: it is character.

—Albert Einstein (1879–1955)

If you can surround a person with a new culture, a different web of relationships, then they will absorb new habits of thought and behaviors.

—David Brooks, 2011

If we want our children to possess the traits of character we most admire, we need to teach them what those traits are and why they deserve both admiration and allegiance. Children must learn to identify the forms and content of those traits.

—William J. Bennett, former US secretary of education

When we first began to lay the foundations for the Validation Program, we weren't sure how youngsters could begin to look outside themselves, to see others through an other-oriented focus. Nor were we clear how to go about getting them to become positive with one another. Certainly lecturing about the notions of looking for the good in others—and how to develop empathy, understanding, and acceptance—doesn't ensure a genuinely motivated change or impact. Enough lecturing has been done for decades.

Should we buy prepackaged, mass-marketed programs suggesting instant results? Research has yet to suggest such approaches have had a positive long-term impact on the characteristics we were looking for. Should we ask students to write individual "all about me" stories or descriptions? Play "get to know me and each other" games? Watch marketing videos telling us "how to be kind and caring in twelve weeks"? We weren't sure then, but are now even more suspect that such approaches work out. (John Bradshaw, a scholar in psychology and philosophy and a professional counselor, pinpoints a curt reminder about how we acquire virtues: they "can't be taught from the outside through instruction" [Bradshaw, 2009]).

All we instinctively knew was that we should design the program from the child up so each youngster could personally and genuinely focus on one another while simultaneously looking for the positive in the other. This approach provides youngsters the most likely means of genuine learning and supports the leaning theory that when learners own and are personally engaged in the construction, process, and development of the program, they are more likely to truly learn whatever we want them to learn. Ultimately, they learn the components of what constitutes good character: the virtues, values, ethics, and dispositions of being a good human being.

Then it happened. By chance we met two American educators at a conference in the Netherlands, a husband and wife team, Gerry and Margaret Schiele, teaching in a small school in Germany. They explained how they had found a successful way to affirm students' worth at a workshop, and it sounded like the notion we were after. They referred to it as "validation." Since then, the Validation Program you find in this book has undergone significant revision and refinement. The Validation Program's changes and alterations are a result of thirty-five years of study, practice, research, reflection, and fine-tuning.

In 1976 the Schieles invited us to bring our students to their school to observe the Validation Program. So we boarded our students, staff, and some parents on a train and went to their two-teacher school near the North Sea in Germany. After eating a spaghetti dinner at the school, sleeping in sleeping bags on the gym floor, taking a fishing boat ride on the North Sea, and observing the validation process in their school, we boarded a train back to Uden and started our own Validation Program.

Validation pairs each child with another child on a weekly basis. This places students in an other-oriented role, connecting one-on-one with each other. As they sincerely defined the good in each other, within the context of the group as a whole, we hoped we would see definite impacts on their attitudes and behavior toward others. We knew we would need to structure the program to provide a framework that would be easy to comprehend, simple to implement, and something students would enjoy.

The rest is history. We began the Validation Program in our little two-teacher elementary school in 1976 in the south central part of the Netherlands, Uden American School. Thirty-five years later, after sharing the program with hundreds of K–12 educators in workshops across the United States and Europe, many teachers have incorporated the Validation Program into their classrooms as a significant part of their curriculum.

As David Brooks says, "Character emerges gradually out of the mysterious interplay of good influences" and "emphasizes the power of small and repetitive action to rewire the fundamental mechanisms of the brain. Aristotle was right when he observed, 'We acquire virtues by first having put them into action'" (Brooks, 2011).

Describing the Validation Program

You gotta accentuate the positive, eliminate the negative, latch on to the affirmative, and don't mess with Mr. In Between.

—Harold Arlen and Johnny Mercer

While not necessarily the foremost outcomes sought when implementing the Validation Program, teachers can professionally and academically reference it as a part of the language arts curriculum.

First comes the written part—writing a weekly validation for one's assigned partner. As a student, pretend you and I are partners this week. Our task is to write a "validation" for each other. You write good and true things about me, and I write good and true things about you. Both of us do so without fabricating, patronizing, humoring, or otherwise being false about each other. (These latter points are some of the operational expectations explained and established early in the program with students and teachers, and discussed later—among additional implementation components of the program.)

Second and third come the reading and speaking parts: reading our validations aloud, speaking directly to each other. Lastly, listening became a significant part of the language arts curriculum, and one of the biggest surprises to us. Not only did joy occur within the partners as they listened closely to their validations, the whole class listened rather intensely with a sense of connection and attention unlike we'd seen before. As you can predict, when the other classmates listen attentively to all the good and positive attributes of each classmate, their perceptions of themselves, their partners, and others listening change for the good.

Toward the end of the week we gather together as a class. You and I (as well as all the other classroom validation partners) read our prepared validations, one at a time, aloud to each other, at the front of the classroom or gathering place. Yep, we stand facing one another, reading aloud our compositions to one another as the rest of the class watches and listens. Then the teacher calls out the next pair of students, and so on, until everyone has shared their validations.

Afterward, as a resulting component, the teacher facilitates a "synthesis session," similar to a coaching summation. The teacher summarizes, offers suggestions, and reinforces special, insightful comments. Because we learned later that students were excited to know who would be their next week's partner, teachers will sometime later choose to announce next week's paired partners before they head on to the next school activity or lesson.

A. A Program and a Nurturing Construct

A lot of people in this English class are thought of as "nerds" or "nosers." I used to avoid them. But after I validated them or watched them validate someone else, I began to see all their kindness and care pour out.

—Twelfth-grade student

Validation can be conceptualized simultaneously as both a program and a nurturing construct. The two are interlinked. The "program" part is like any program. At an instructional level, validation is a language-centered program where students write, read, speak, and listen to one another in a real setting, for real and sincere purposes. It is a specific intervention program with several parts and components—all described in this book spelling out the functional components of the program.

Simultaneously, validation is a nurturing construct. What we've learned is that it becomes a—if not "the"—major function of the program. The nurturing construct outlines and reinforces the goals that help students begin to develop an other-oriented perspective rather than the all-too-common narcissistic view of themselves.

Many other goals are also embedded within the program: a greater understanding of others, acceptance, tolerance, empathy, and compassion. The development of students' positive perspectives toward their classmates and toward life in general gradually evolves. Validation reinforces character development through a genuine other-oriented perspective, resulting in unity, bonding, caring, and harmony. As a nurturing construct, validation serves as a catalyst for the healthy conceptualization and confirmation of self, others, and the surrounding culture.

Validation is a rich alternative to a number of different activities intended to enhance positive, other-oriented perspectives. (We have all seen a number of well-intentioned but too often external superficial attempts to solidify sound character development: "Student of the Month," "All about Me" posters, or other snazzy commercial programs advertised in catalogs or periodicals.)

B. The Language of Validation

Through the words spoken and written in validations, students regularly hear and later read the abundant positive attributes about themselves. The language of validation identifies, describes, and defines the multifaceted and multidimensional parts of the self. Validations become the descriptive and definitive mirrors of the self. As someone once said, "We are what we believe about what we are told."

For example, one student tells his partner, Mark, "You're a good reader." Next week a different student tells Mark, "You help us keep the room calm." As such descriptions reach Mark's ears and eyes week after week, as he hears over and over the positive descriptions others have written about him, as he stockpiles his validations month after month—sharing them with his parents and friends, rereading them again and again—his validation repertoire helps build solid, clear, and positive perceptions of himself and others. His and his partners' self-concepts are broadened unlike ever before.

Validation also provides discovery opportunities for one's self-concept, self-realization, self-esteem, self-actualization, self-efficacy, and self-worth. When we have the chance to hear and see how others perceive us, we learn new things about ourselves—things we hadn't known existed.

We hear how someone thinks we are intelligent, skilled, gentle, patient, kind, and generous. (See sample students' comments in Appendix A.) We hear someone refer to us like a brother, a sister, a friend—comments we seldom ever heard before.

Because the discoveries about ourselves are all positive, we glow with the wonder and delight of hearing something good about ourselves—something we might hear later in life or not at all. But it might be heard at our funeral.

Over time, all students begin to learn that all class members have defined each other in positive, healthy ways. In return, they find they grow more favorable toward one another. The more they know they are liked, the more they like each other. The more they like each other, the more they bond. And the more they bond, the more empathic and compassionate they become.

Because validation occurs weekly, students begin to see themselves as regularly valued. Their self-worth is bolstered, reinforced, and sustained. The behavioral vice of bullying diminishes. Together, students become more wholesome and connected. A sense of oneness begins to occur, and together everyone takes the first fundamental steps toward harmony, unity, compassion, and peace.

C. Celebrating the Differences: A Mosaic of Understanding

> I'm sixteen and don't enjoy school, so I kind of rebel against programs no matter what they are. I do think [validation] has helped me though. I find talking with the kids in my class easier, and I enjoy being in their company more. I also feel a little better about myself, and it has helped me find the confidence to try new things that otherwise I would be afraid to, like trying to learn how to play the guitar.
>
> —Twelfth-grade student

Validation provides youngsters another opportunity—a realistic opportunity to celebrate our differences. Children and adults have had few realistic opportunities to celebrate each other's differences. We learn to appreciate and respect others by not insisting we all be the same. We begin to notice there is diversity in all of us and that the classroom is filled with all these metaphorical artists who add to the beauty of life, creating a sense of oneness. When we recognize this, we have a better sense of tolerance for one another.

As an aside, one illustration of the appreciation for the differences in others has been manifested in some of the validations students prepare. I remember visiting one classroom of sixth graders. Two students, Christina and Laura, came up to the front of the room. I watched Christina face Laura, who got on her knees with a box in her hands. Out of the box she picked up a long, cardboard microphone covered with aluminum foil and read her validation. At the end she sang a song to Laura, even though she laughed a little while doing so. The song was about Laura growing up to be a model.

Another student, Stephanie, informed her partner that she had written a play. She called it "The Brown Paper Bag Show." She pulled out individual slips of paper from the paper bag with her validation comments written thereon. As she read the slips of paper, she squeezed her nose to make the bag character very distinct, an example of how some students become very creative.

Yet her validation comments were as sincere and genuine as they would have been had she just written a single paper validation.

> All our lives, we search for ways to satisfy our needs for love, belonging, caring, sharing, and cooperation. If a student feels no sense of belonging in school, no sense of being involved in caring and concern, that child will pay little attention to academic subjects.

> —William Glasser

D. The Practical Considerations

Incorporating the Validation Program into the curriculum does not automatically suggest teachers change the way they conduct their classrooms. Yet validation has a specific structure providing students with real-life, personally relevant, authentic, and meaning-centered approaches to defining and reinforcing their strengths, abilities, and capabilities. Validation is a foundation builder, a source of stability and growth. When teachers begin to implement the program, they will discover how to do so. They will learn the techniques and strategies (outlined later) for successfully implementing the program, all of which are critical to the success of the program.

Classrooms are typically populated with a kaleidoscope of students, all with ongoing needs for recognition, self-worth, and belonging. Teachers are keen to provide students with meaningful opportunities to feel valued and significant. Yet there are few personally relevant programs that permit students opportunities to use their own language and thoughts to connect with one another in supportive and sincere ways.

A practical consideration for any classroom is to help educators find ways to uplift students. Validation uplifts classrooms, the school climate and culture, the community, families, and faculty members as well.

What follows is information about how to implement the program. There is no mystical formula. The teacher is the students' primary education model and first-line leader in the school. The required ingredient is a fundamental belief that all children learn best and live best knowing they are valued and cared for. And as children become positive and accepting of each other, they begin to develop a sense of community, as well as a sense of responsibility for the welfare, goodness, and unity of the members of their communities.

Of course what we realized is that as students learned how to become other-oriented and positive toward one another, they began to believe in themselves, to see themselves as good humans who are valued. As they look, they see. And as they see, they learn about the "human goods," the virtues so critical to positive character. These outcomes may not happen for all students, but if we can make a beginning with some of them, we can take small steps toward peace—personally, community-wide, and worldwide.

The Basic Organization

No psychological health is possible unless the essential core of the person is fundamentally accepted, loved, and respected by others and himself.

—Abraham H. Maslow

A. Who Participates in Validation?

Everyone in the classroom participates, and because the teacher is a vital "significant other" in the lives of students, he or she always participates as a partner with a student. The modeling opportunities here are powerful. The teacher has the chance to demonstrate not only the other-oriented focus but a well-written validation, the thoughtful delivery of the validation, and an appreciative response to being uplifted by validations. (In fact, teachers often report they are delightfully pleased about what their students think of them, and they find they like their students even more.)

Depending upon the structure and philosophy of the school, other members of the school or classroom community (administrators, school resource officers, volunteers, nurses, lunchroom monitors, secretaries, counselors, etc.) are also encouraged to join the class for weekly validation sessions. In several schools, they rotate regularly as validation partners with one of the students. Significant others always abound inside and outside the school.

Additionally, the participation of important adults in the program dignifies the whole idea of validation for the students. As the validation program becomes part of the school culture, each adult's validation helps strengthen the foundation for what is valued throughout society.

Validation, then, begins to serve as an agent that enhances the expected, operational norms and ethos of the school.

The tone validation sets for the school has a driving force of its own. Human behavior in school is shaped by the social, interactive influences of validation. As classrooms define again and again the characteristics of good people, it is no surprise that the classrooms, and the school, begin to develop an ethos and culture of a respectful community of learners. School psychologists, secretaries, custodians, and even school bus drivers have joined students for validation sessions. Who eventually participates in the validation process and weekly sessions depends on your horizons, your school's structure, and of course what you believe you can manage and the school supports.

> In the arena of human life, the honors and rewards fall to those who show their good qualities in action.
>
> —Aristotle

B. Identifying/Determining Validation Partners

At the beginning of every week in a many classrooms, the teacher usually starts by reading out the list of paired partners for that week, referred to as "validation partners." The following week each student is paired with a different partner, and so on, week after week. Where practical, encouraging other school personnel and community members to participate promotes the notion of community oneness.

When to Pair. Not long after students are introduced and experience the validation sessions, they will often ask, "Who's my next validation partner?" They are curious and excited. Many teachers announce the pairing at the beginning of the week, but as mentioned earlier, some teachers let students know their next week's partners immediately after validation time and the synthesis session.

How to Pair. Teachers can randomly pair students by simply drawing names out of a hat.

This is initially an easy approach and may work well the first four to five weeks. However, it soon becomes time-consuming and complex because you will run head-on into duplications of students who have already validated one another.

It is easier to manage if names are pre-paired by the teacher (or a teacher assistant or parent helper). Some sort of record keeping and pre-paired planning is essential to track pairings and to avoid duplications or potential complications. Various teachers develop a chart of sorts to schedule and keep track of all student pairings.

Partnering for Success. When initially pairing students, pair them for success. Because you will want to ensure the first validation session goes well, it is critical to pre-pair each student with those students you know will be able to validate each other comfortably and successfully.

We all have students who offer special challenges. Pair these students with a student you know will help them validate comfortably and successfully the first time. If you know for example that John has been having difficulty with Mark, don't pair them initially. If Jennifer is not well liked by some of the students in the class, have her be your validation partner, or put her with someone you know can give her a positive validation. If you validate Jennifer, you'll demonstrate to the whole class right away that there are abundant good and true things about Jennifer that can be identified. In so doing, you model for the entire class that everyone is valuable and expected to find good and true things about one another no matter who they are. Later, when validation becomes more established, youngsters will accept your random pairings as a matter of course.

Additionally, some teachers arrange for their student partners to sit together just after they have been assigned and interview one another. Another teacher informed her students that they were to sit together at some specific lunchtime to chat and get to know their partners more prior to composing their validations.

C. The Two Key Guidelines

When validation is introduced to students, we make it a bit easier by telling them there are only two guidelines to follow when preparing a validation. We say to students, "Everything you write and say about your validation partner must be *good* and *true*." These are the only two guidelines we provide students in the beginning. (Suggestion: resist using the word *rules*. Some students may perceive *rules* as having negative connotations.) We have found it less confusing and nonthreatening to offer only these two guidelines.

However, it is necessary to provide definitions for these two guidelines. Experience has taught us that we need to explain what is meant by the words "good" and "true." Early explanations help students know precisely what is expected when we talk about validations being "good" and "true" documentations of their partners.

We begin by talking about the word "good." We explain "good" as being those comments which are positive, nice, exceptional, noteworthy, or splendid about a person. The "good" can be what a person is or can do. For example, "You are kind and considerate," or "You are good at math (or geography or writing, etc.)."

We also learned it was necessary to illustrate that all "good" comments must be 100 percent good. We ask students to be careful as they prepare their good comments, so that no negative (or half-good) statements creep in. Sometimes we actually practice examples aloud with students, particularly younger students, providing them a variety of sample comments. For example, as a half-good, half-not-so-good comment, we might say, "You are kind on the playground, most of the time." Continued reminders will likely be needed to help students be careful when writing their validations. Steer students away from the use of qualifiers like "sometimes," "most of the time," "usually," and so on.

You may find a rare student who "slips," or slides in a snide remark bordering on the "not good" side or clearly negative side. If this happens (depending on the severity of the comment) the teacher can discuss this during the synthesis session at the end of the validation time—or talk with the student privately afterward. Help the student understand the violation that has just occurred and kindly address this issue. Inform the student that most, if not all, the students in the classroom are well aware of this slip. It may also be a good idea to let the student know he or she needs to apologize to the partner and that you are going to schedule a time for all three of you to meet for this apology session.

Additionally, it is necessary to explain what is meant by "true." Students will need reminding that they are not to fabricate comments about their partners. We've found it helps to say something like, "Please do not make up things to say about your partner for any reason," and if they do, "I will chat with you individually and privately about it." They need to know that to obtain valid information for their validations you expect them to employ any of the following approaches: watch their partner, observe, look for the good things said or done, listen, and talk to or interview the partner or their friends.

Sometimes we ask students how they can find the good and true things about their partners. Usually they come up with a list as good as any we prepare in advance. Some students quickly relate that simply interviewing their partner will help. Sometimes in the beginning teachers use the interview technique, scheduling time for students to interview each other before writing validations. This technique can be helpful in the beginning.

> Fame is a vapor, popularity an accident, riches take wing, and only character endures.
>
> —Horace Greeley, American journalist and educator (1811–72)

D. Caution: "Beauty Is in the Eye of the Beholder."

Experience has also taught us, especially with older students, that we have to ask them to be careful about judging other people's validations in terms of their own personal perceptions. At this point, we've found it helpful to talk about beauty being in the eye of the beholder, as well as the self-fulfilling prophecy.

As students listen to others' validations, we ask them to be careful about saying to themselves, "But that's not what I think." We remind them that what one person sees in another may not always be what a third person sees. We explain that each person has a right to his or her perceptions, even when those perceptions contradict our own.

We ask each partner to be genuine and honest as each looks for the things that are true. The overwhelming majority of students meet this expectation. If it is violated (and it will be, somewhere along the way), approach the student privately and reflect on the perception or observation together. Not all students automatically know how to look for or find the good and true in others. They will likely need your individual guidance.

In an indirect way, validation can manifest itself as a self-fulfilling prophecy for many students. When youngsters begin to define each other in good and positive ways (ways sometimes not evident to others, or even to the child himself or herself), we've witnessed them begin to see themselves the way their peers define them. Like a metamorphosis, some students begin to adopt the traits others so powerfully see in them.

As suggested earlier, validation becomes a catalyst for establishing classroom and school climate. "What's important" becomes the cultural norm for the classroom and school.

> I'm sure validation is good for younger kids too, but I think for our age group it's much better. We know how to express our feelings in more depth than we did while we were small. Friends at our age are usually much closer so we know more about them. It really boosts people's confidence. It sure makes me feel good. All of our class now knows a lot more about each other; therefore, we are a lot closer. I hope we can keep this up!
>
> —Twelfth-grade student

E. Where Does Validation Occur?

We have found that validation—the event—has occurred in a number of different settings. There is no limit on where it can occur. It can occur in self-contained classrooms, in any of the subject area classrooms, in homerooms, and in resource rooms. In Europe, we even found the program popping up in foreign-language classrooms.

Validation occurs in large and small groups, even in one-on-one sessions between a student and an administrator, or a student and counselor, especially for some special-needs youngsters, or those extremely shy or who otherwise find validation awkward in the beginning. When the validation process becomes part of the school culture, it can occur anywhere. Students have reported conducting their own validation sessions in student council meetings, computer clubs, and on overnight field trips. In these latter cases, it is encouraging to learn that no adult made the decision to hold a validation session elsewhere. Significant impact has been made when the validation process becomes a catalytic force outside the school. It is reassuring and exciting to learn of families who voluntarily implement the validation process in their homes at specific times.

I vividly recall one family's excursion into validation. The father, an air force lieutenant colonel, explained the first time his family decided to try validation at home. It was directly after his three daughters, ages eight, ten, and thirteen, erupted into an argument. Since he and his wife knew their daughters had written validations for other students at school, they decided that under the present circumstances, validation would be worth putting to the test at home. Mom and Dad sent their three daughters to their bedrooms to write validations for each other.

While this type of implementation may not always work, it did on this and subsequent occasions. The father and mother were so moved by the results of their daughters' efforts (and eventual restoration of harmony and resulting goodwill), they announced they would all prepare and present validations as a family to each other every month. At home, this family made validation part of their lifestyle.

The self is built almost entirely, if not entirely, in relationship to others. The crucial matter is not so much what you are but what you think you are.

—Earl C. Kelley

F.   Where Are Validations Written and When Are They Presented?

As a prelude to this section, from the teachers' and students' perspectives, it is helpful to explain or illustrate that validation is both a product and an event. That is, it is a piece of student writing, the validation itself, and it is an event, typically called "Validation Time," when students and teachers participate as givers and receivers of written validations.

After pairings are established, sometime during the week each partner prepares a written validation. Teachers often ask, "When and where are validations written?" Strongly encourage students to write their validations outside class, especially since it is a perfect activity to do at home, where they can do so in their own domain, in private and at a time they choose. When you stress this point, most students comply.

Also ask students to kindly reflect on and seriously consider hand writing their validations. We know that hand writing skills are diminishing and we understand the convenience of using a computer. But there are other obvious reasons for legible handwriting in this world. In any case, you might want to share with students the research that has found, "Brain scans show that handwriting engages more sections of the brain than typing" (Begley, 2012).

As validation takes hold, you will find some students automatically beginning their validations when they see a free moment in school and finishing them at home. Some begin them at home and finish them in school. Both approaches build positive home-school connections. If students know this expectation, and know that they are to have their validations finished by the time the teacher specifies, the majority will be prepared.

In reality, some students (for various reasons) will not write it at home, even though it is an opportune out-of-school activity. You might be tempted to begin having students write their initial validations in class. If you do so, continue to promote writing validations outside class. Remind students that taking individual private time to think and prepare their validations is only fair to themselves and their partners. You and your students have enough on your plates during the day anyway, and time is precious.

As far as when you want to require students to have their validations finished and in the classroom, you might want to say something to the students like, "Please be sure all validations are brought to school by Wednesday" (or whatever day you decide). Even under such stipulations, you may find some students who do not have their Validations ready or written. In such cases you may want to consider giving them time (during recess, down time or some other time) to write their Validation. Or you may want to give them another day to write theirs at home. For students who might need assistance, there are always volunteers who will help if asked, even to take dictation.

We have found it ideal to end the week with validations. That decision may be yours or the school's. When students end the week with validations, they feel "up." What a great way to end the school week. Students have even reported that they look forward to coming back to school on Monday because they want to find out who their next validation partner will be for the following week.

Preschoolers and kindergartners sometimes validate their partners orally (and/or in some visual, artistic way), monitored by the teacher or aid, either of whom may transcribe what kindergartners say into print. In one class, the kindergarten teacher uses a tape recorder to record what the children say and later transcribes their remarks via a computer onto paper. Another kindergarten teacher has a separate theme each week: a flower garden, ice-cream cones, or hats. From a variety of colored construction paper, the student and/or teacher cuts out various shapes. While students say good and true things to their partners sitting or standing nearby, the teacher writes down the notable expressions on various pieces of paper. Students later glue or paste their comments on the background paper and present their validations to their partners.

By now, you have probably already asked yourself, "What about those students who don't have their validations ready?" Admittedly, at some point there will be those who aren't prepared. That's why we provide early, solid expectations and cautions about the "pitfalls" of validation (see the "pitfalls" section below). Early, solid expectations allay most problems. Our experience has taught us that the teacher always finds a way of coping with this problem when it occurs.

So if you anticipate this possibility as a serious problem, you might start off by having students write validations in class, if there is time. In any case, every student must be solidly informed that all are expected to prepare a validation.

Steering Students around the Possible Pitfalls

A stumble may prevent a fall.

—Thomas Fuller II

When introducing validation to students, we have found it critical to explain that validation works best when some of the pits, into which they might slip, are avoided.

You can visually display the meaning of a pitfall for younger students by walking two fingers along an imaginary road. Students' eyes follow walking fingers easily as you talk about how things in life oftentimes go well, until we slip and stumble into a pit. At which point your fingers plunge into an imaginary pit. Visually, such a simple illustration prepares students for the point you want to make—that there are some pits they must avoid before they begin validation. The reason you share these pitfalls is to provide them advance warning.

After you identify the pits (and if you do not care for the word *pits*, you could also call them *obstacles* or *blockades*), remind students not to be disappointed or cross with you when you notice or identify that they have slipped and/or stumbled into any one of the pits. You have given them advance warning.

Share these pitfalls to minimize the possible complications or mishaps that can occur, steering them around or over the pits. Depending on the sophistication and maturity level of your students, some pitfalls (as well as some of the suggested points in this article) will be more relevant than others for certain age groups. You might find it helpful to compile and display a "Possible Pitfall Pile List" (or something to that effect) they may face along the way.

When you choose to introduce the possible pitfalls is up to you. To avoid possible "mind wandering," you might want to introduce the pitfalls separately at some other time. Explaining the entirety of the program in one single session may be a bit of a challenge for them and you.

> Life is like playing a violin in public and learning the instrument as one goes on.
>
> —Samuel Butler (1835–1902)

Pitfall #1: Forgetting

Of all pitfalls, this one is usually the most needling. Some students will sincerely forget their validations and others will provide excuses. Some will claim their bratty brother threw it away. Some will whine their little sister scribbled on it. Others will explain (with some truth) that their parents sent them to bed early for being naughty, and it didn't get written. Justifiable exceptions aside, communicate the expectation that each validation partner is required to have her or his validation ready on the day they're due. Certainly there are reasons that demand flexibility. And such flexibility is sometime necessary, while keeping the integrity of the expectation intact. By establishing this pitfall as a firm expectation to avoid, you'll find students will less likely forget their validations.

When introducing this pitfall, it might be helpful to ask students to put themselves in the other person's shoes for a moment. Ask them to pretend it is "Validation Time" and they have worked hard to prepare their validation for their partner. You might say something like, "You have taken a lot of time and prepared a well-thought-out, well-written validation." In fact, I heard a teacher once say that "a well-written valuation is a hundred-dollar validation." (You may not want to illustrate validation with a quantitative value to reinforce the notion that validations are important. You might fear that attaching a tangible extrinsic "award" value sends the wrong message.)

"Picture yourself," you continue, "standing in front of the class, facing your partner, ready to share your validation. And there you are, face to face with a partner who has 'forgotten' his or her validation. How do you feel knowing you have taken lots of time to prepare your validation and your partner doesn't have one for you?" Students readily respond. "I'd think the person doesn't like me," or "I'd be disappointed," or "I'd feel hurt." Some say they would be angry. You might want to take this approach for them to own what it means.

Next, you might ask them to pretend they are the person who has, for some reason or another, "forgotten" his or her validation. Ask them to tell you how they feel now, standing face to face with their partner who has written a fine validation, while theirs has been "forgotten." They readily supply obvious answers: "I'd feel embarrassed," or "Dumb," or "Like I want to crawl away somewhere."

You might also take this scenario one step further and ask how they think the teacher or their other classmates might feel about the person who has slipped into this pit. Their responses will be honest. Placing students through this exercise when you introduce them to the validation process helps sensitize them to the unfair position they can put others and themselves in when they "forget" their validations.

Of course, one of the reasons for asking students to put themselves in the other person's shoes for a moment is to practice empathy and underscore the importance of being reliable and responsible to one's partner, the class, the teacher, and oneself. Asking students to project themselves into what might be a bit awkward or uncomfortable moments (especially for middle and high-school students who have had no previous experience with validation before), may be the stimuli to help them seriously consider the importance of being prepared, and to avoid embarrassing or awkward moments. This kind of imagining is a way of reaching out to others in considerate, caring ways, reinforcing the importance of social responsibility.

While peer pressure, sound expectations, and standing in front of one's entire class may serve to motivate students to come prepared with a validation, it is no guarantee students will always be prepared. However, if we don't emphasize this potential pitfall and establish firm expectations to avoid it, we can expect (what we have learned to be) the inevitable: a recurring headache of "forgotten" validations.

You may want to share an example of what one student had to say when he realized one of his classmates said he "forgot" his validation. "You forgot your validation? That's like leaving your head at home!"

Pitfall #2: "Oh No! Not a (Boy or Girl)!"

Some youngsters, particularly the less mature and less secure, may wade into this sexist and unjustifiable pitfall.

As we introduce this pitfall, we usually write on the board, "Oh no! Not a _____," omitting the word *boy* or *girl*. We do this in advance as an attention device, letting students supply the appropriate pronoun in the blank when the time comes. You might say to students, for example, "Whenever validation partners are announced on Mondays, I will be looking around the room at your eyes, your facial expressions, and behaviors to tell me whether you are slipping into this pit, or some other unpleasant reaction or situation."

You might say something like this: "Here's the way I can tell if you are beginning to fall into this pit. Let's pretend it's Monday morning and we announce who your validation partner is for the week. If you are a fellow and your validation partner is a girl, inside your brain some of you may be thinking, *Oh no! Not a girl.* And if you're a girl, and you get a guy, some of you might think, *Oh no! Not a boy.* Now, you are smarter than to say this out loud. But sometimes we can see it in your eyes or in your face by the expressions you make. Sometimes you slip and make snide vocal responses. Sometimes you are tempted to giggle or laugh. Sometimes you roll your eyes. The point is, this is all unfair and shows an undesirable bias. Even though you might find it awkward at first to be paired with a boy if you're a girl, or with a girl if you are a boy, it is still unfair to make such a sexist response."

We continue to underline the notion of equality and justice by explaining to students that in this classroom and this school, one thing we want everyone to understand is that we all treat each other as important, worthy, and equal. Many teachers in the past have said something like this: "Sure I may be taller than you, older than you. I may come from a different country or state, have different skin color, and talk differently. But we are all to be respectful to each other. I am no better than you and you are no better than I am."

Just as we value our diversities, we also talk about the quality of respect as a commonly understood principle in our class. We say to students, "This is what we believe in and stand for in this school." When we outline this expectation for students, we do more than simply provide a practical warning in the form of a pitfall for a particular program. We establish the important standards and virtues for responsible and respectful citizenship, and the expected ethos to permeate our classroom and school.

Interestingly enough, younger students seldom slip into this pitfall. Primary grade students typically have little difficulty accepting girls and boys as equals. Consciously, it is probably fair to say most have yet to make any significant internalized, sexist distinctions between the sexes.

We've found older youngsters, however, more sensitive to this issue and likely to slip and display this distinction.

We have a responsibility to curb sexist and other unfair stereotypical attitudes and behaviors and to uphold the responsibility of becoming a good quality human being in our classroom and society. The validation program inherently communicates the attitudes and behaviors expected in your classroom.

Firmly stress the avoidance of this pitfall. Students should know that if they fall into this pit you will confront them privately, reminding them they have slipped. In time, students accept ownership of keeping everyone else on track and help each other avoid all the pitfalls. When students demonstrate this ownership, it is another cause for celebration.

Pitfall #3: "Oh No! I Don't Like (Him or Her)."

This pitfall is similar to pitfall #2. Experience has taught us that some youngsters, either overtly or covertly, fall into this pit, no matter how mature or sophisticated.

When introducing this pitfall to students, like pitfall #2 on the board, you might write, "Oh no! I don't like _____," again leaving the blank empty. As we explain this pitfall, we mention that when students do fall into this pit, they often do so right away.

We ask them to picture what it's like when some students first learn who their validation partners will be for that week. We ask them to picture some of their facial expressions: eyes rolling, awkward glances, and obvious frowns that give them away. We announce that we can especially tell when a student has fallen into this pit because (inside his or her head) he or she says something like, "Oh no! I don't like (him or her). I can't think of anything good to write about (him or her)."

Like pitfall #2, this pitfall is unfair. Since the major guidelines specify we are to write good and true things about our partner, that expectation also suggests we set aside our egos and dislikes.

The important point to emphasize here is that no matter how much we dislike a person, no matter how horrid we think a person may be, there are still good points about that person. Our job is to find those good points, to be a kind of "PD"—"positive detective." We may need to personally interview our partner. We might need to talk to one of our partner's friends, or to the teacher, counselor, or parents. Regardless, our job is to search for good things that are true, not made up. We will need to remind youngsters there are always good and true attributes to be found in everyone. Simply said, validation gives us permission to find the good in everyone. As we find the good and articulate and reinforce the good, the good becomes the norm.

Pitfall #4: No Texting, Tweeting, or Facebooking in Advance.

Given the current and frequent modes of technological communication among our students of various age levels, we need to alert those students likely to fall into this pit.

We can certainly admit that some students will and can write their validations via a word processing program. We can also simultaneously suggest to students, with particular emphasis, that the uniqueness of preparing a handwritten validation is as significant or powerful as what has become too often the norm—a tech-written validation. This suggestion is not intended to forbid or demean a tech-written and printed validation. Even this approach can result in cleverly designed and artistic validations. Asking students to handwrite a validation may be "old fashioned" to them, but it also suggests importance of individual handwriting skills.

However, we do want to particularly emphasize that since the validation is going to be formally presented to one's partner in the classroom, it is to remain private to the writer and the partner until Validation Time.

We suggest addressing this pitfall to students because it is likely to be too tempting in advance to some students to (electronically and secretly) slip their validation to the student (or even other students, friends, etc.) in advance. It is critical to uphold this point because falling into this pitfall may be not only a "spoiler," it is a violation of the integrity and purpose of validation.

You may want to decide whether you would endorse the following option. If after receiving one's validation in the classroom, do you want to let students know whether it is okay for the receiving partner to decide to share his or her validation with others through whatever technology he or she uses? However, you might want to ignore this approach. There is a real likelihood that this kind of comment bolsters an ego-enhancing opportunity for tooting one's own horn of self-obsession.

You might want to acknowledge that since the validation one receives is his or hers to do with whatever he or she wishes, it may be harmful or backfire when "broadcasted" to others. Doing so could run the risk of being in violation of what the writer would expect or want to happen. It could even become a cyberbullying issue if another person or student wanted to be critically defiant or demeaning of what another student says about the goodness of others. The use of technology for this kind of possibility is too easy, if not tempting, to exploit for those with hidden agendas or dislikes.

Because this pitfall is a rather recent one, it could or could not be a troublesome issue. More thought and discussion is advisable before one begins to decide how much or to what extent this is a significant pitfall issue to address.

Pitfall #5: Bestowing Unnecessary, Inappropriate Gifts, Toys, or Other Goodies

Occasionally, students may become so engrossed with the validation notion that they may want to go even beyond the written validation itself, simply because they would like to add something to the written validation. On some occasions in the past, students have felt motivated to give their partner something extra. However, one wonders if they may feel that he or she will be even more liked, or impressive, by going unnecessarily beyond the expected written validation.

When sharing this potential pitfall, you'll probably want to communicate with them that it is understandable that some may feel motivated to do so. But that is not the purpose of validation. It is the written language we want to stress as the means of expressing one's appreciation and kindness toward another. Bestowing added gifts or extra goodies along with the written validation undermines the major focus of the program—to focus singularly on the positive character traits of one's partner.

However, you may find that some students truly enjoy decorating or including some illustrations as they prepare their validations. Most of the time this is simply a fun way to be a little creative and is certainly okay.

Pitfall #6: Being Personally Judgmental

This particular pitfall refers of course to the guideline that all validations are to be true. And in sharing this guideline with students in the beginning, it may be helpful to reinforce it by considering the following.

There will be times when students might make statements about their partner that seem (to other students and to you) untrue. In your synthesis sessions, you may find a need, on some occasions, to remind students of this guideline. However, it could well be that in some instances, the student actually believes his or her partner possess a quality that we, as educators, do not see in that child.

When this does occur, it is probably more important to generally remind students not to be the one to judge whether a person has this quality. We have actually learned that sometimes when one person sees in another what appears to be evidence of a particular quality, skill, trait, or behavior that we don't see, it could be a positive occurrence. It could actually have a beneficial effect. I might even begin to be more motivated to strive for a particular quality that one sees within me.

If you consider this pitfall unnecessary or not timely initially, you certainly may want to omit it.

Pitfall #7: Use of First-Person Singular Pronouns

This is a simple reminder that when writing and reading one's validation, it is important to use the pronoun "you," rather than the pronouns "I, he, or she."

Although this pitfall is not an egregious one, it is a good idea to let students know in advance they are writing a validation directly to their partner, especially for that partner, not for the public. This is a minor slip but one that will help students comprehend that the comments are to be directed specifically to and for their partners.

It takes two to speak the truth—one to speak and another to hear.

—Henry David Thoreau

Conclusion

If you treat an individual as he is, he will stay as he is. But if you treat him as if he were what he ought to be and could be, he will become what he ought to be and could be.

—Goethe

For educators, parents, caretakers, counselors, and many others, our pedagogical expertise, knowledge, and skills help our youngsters acquire the basic education to understand life in all its glory. The fire of education must never be watered down or extinguished, nor should it shortchange youngsters' whole-child development.

Validations, at least when first started, may be short but telling. After students regularly receive their validations over a sustained period of time (the longer the better), students' characters and emotional intelligence grow. As the validation experiences are repeated over and over, the brain develops strengthened pathways that reinforce what is most crucial to our future than ever before—the ability to be decent human beings.

We have a responsibility to model and teach the qualities of good human beings, the virtues. Teaching is an ongoing effort of faith; faith that our efforts and guidance can help our students maximize the traits of good character and develop positive relationships with one another. As we work to help our students see that when they behave according to the various virtues they learn, it is like handing a star to another person.

Since parents entrust their youngsters to us, as trustees we are not just responsible for helping children acquire academic backgrounds. We also serve as exemplars and guardians of respectful behavior. Are we aware of the qualities of character we embody and pass along to students?

Our daily challenge will always be to have extraordinary victories over ignorance and defunct character. Our continued professional reflection, knowledge, experience, and commitment to enrich sound minds and character will be with us throughout our lives.

Children develop character by what they see, what they hear, and what they are repeatedly led to do.

—James Stenson, "Character in Action"

It has become a significant reality that the biggest impact on the success of the validation program will be you, the implementer. Without your total commitment and perseverance, the program will not have as huge an impact on everyone. It is not a one-shot program done now and then a few times. It is your ongoing dedication that makes a huge difference.

Reflect back now and then on Joel Barker's little story "The Star Thrower." This is the story about a wise man who was walking down the beach one day. In the distance he saw a human figure moving like a dancer. As he got closer, he could see it was a young man, but he wasn't dancing. He was bending down, picking up something, and throwing it into the ocean. As he got closer, he asked the young man what he was doing. The young man explained he was throwing starfish into the ocean. The wise man asked, "Why are you throwing starfish into the ocean?" The young man explained that the sun was up and the tide was going out and that if he didn't throw the starfish in the ocean, they would die. Perplexed, the wise man in his logical wisdom said, "Young man, don't you realize there are miles and miles of beach with starfish all along it? You can't possibly make a difference." The young man listened politely, bent down, threw another starfish into the sea, and said, "It made a difference for that one!"

The young man's action replicates what educators believe: that there is something special in each of our students, and we have the ability to make a difference. We can begin the pathway to shape the future for the good. And if the Validation Program can make a difference to just one youngster, it's worth it.

Efforts have been made to include most of the key components, suggestions, and ideas surrounding the implementation of this program. Here's trusting all this information is not overwhelming. Yet you may condense, revise, expand, or abbreviate the program based on your own teaching practices. You and your students will grow into the program, and most will thank you later, even years later. But only you can bring this about. The key is simply to just *begin* the program. The results will reveal themselves over time, and you will have reinforced the reason you decided to become a teacher—because you *care*.

> If I had to write all the good things about you, I would have to hire someone to write all of it because I would die before I could finish.
>
> —Sixth-grade student to partner

> I think my life would be very different without a validation at the end of the week. I think validations should be introduced to schools around the world.
>
> —Twelfth-grade English honors student

Appendix A

Sample Written Statements Students Have Made to Their Partners

Over the years, thousands of students' validation written comments have been recorded by teachers and other observers. Many can be said to be "ordinary" comments—although students receiving such comments would hardly refer to them as "ordinary." (If someone said you were indeed a considerate or nice person, would you think, *Oh, that's just an "ordinary" comment?*)

There are many, many thoughtful, clever, creative, genuinely touching validation statements students have written about their partners. You are probably thinking that the younger a student happens to be the less impressive, articulate, or literary their comments might be. Many times that is true. But you will likely be surprised by some of their creative, thoughtful remarks. The impacts of their "young" positive comments are just as powerful to students as a very mature and experienced classmate reading her or his validation to an older classmate.

Student-to-Student Written Validation Statements (K–12)

Your love for history is so strong you'll go down in a history book.

You are a nice, caring person. One of my BFFLs (Best Friends For Life).

You make every conversation interesting because you have facts and information that is interesting.

You are responsible. Everyone is glad you are in our class. People can trust you.

You are a gem. You learn to open each new door with a positive mind.

You are like a brother—one of my best buddies, a hard worker, an intelligent person.

You are the type of person who brings happiness to everyone. You don't bring others down.

I'm glad I come to you whenever I need help or just a smile.

You are very loyal, determined, and put your mind to things.

When you ask a question it is like a fishing net going out.

I think you are the coolest person in the world because you know how to stay out of the limelight. That's why I look up to you.

You don't hurt other people's feelings. You brighten up our class.

You remind me of a garden. You are nicer than a rose.

You are charitable and radiant. I wish you could stay with us forever.

You remind me of the song "Happiness." I can't even create a number big enough to tell you how much I like you.

You do your work like a magic bunny.
You are undaunted, unique, and considerate.
You remind me of a ball of sunshine.
I wish your face could be on a penny.
Butterflies are beautiful but not like you.
You are a good dictionary. When we listen to you we hear an intelligent person.
If someone needed a friend they would turn to you.
I am sure your parents are impressed with your work.
When I was sick and not feeling well, I would think of you and feel brand new.
If you were a flower, I would take you to wear on my suit. I would give you the purest water.
(Note: This last comment is one I actually heard at a validation session and will never forget. It was a fourth grader validating her second-grade sister.)

Samples of Student-to-Teacher Validation Comments (K–12)

You are a very good teacher, and I hope you realize my grades don't reflect your teaching skills.
You know how to get material in our brains. You don't ever have anything bad to say about a person.
You thrive on challenging yourself. The lives you touch are greatly benefited.
You are the type of person who brings happiness to everyone. You are dedicated.
You are a strict teacher. You won't let me get away with anything.
You are a terrific teacher and person. You are modest, articulate, sensible, and have a special brain.

The true test of civilization is not the census, nor the size of cities, nor the crops— no, but the kind of person the country turns out.

—Ralph Waldo Emerson

Additional Student Comments about the Impacts of Validation

As you read some of the students' evaluative comments about the impact, success, and positive results of the Validation Program, look for a few that particularly grab you while reflecting on their uniqueness or significance.

These comments were selected from a small number of 270 statements eighth-grade students wrote after their first semester experiencing the Validation Program at Louisa County Middle School in Virginia in 2011. After reading these comments, which are qualitative evidence in themselves, the positive impacts and significance of the program become evident.

Eighth-Grade Student Evaluation Comments

"You realize how great people really are!" "It's very good because a lot of people say mean things, but being told nice things makes you feel good about yourself." "It can make someone's day and boost their confidence." "The program brings students together in many positive ways and makes a way for everyone's light to shine." "I didn't use to have good self-esteem, but when I heard all the things people had noticed about me, I became a new person." "I learned I wasn't an ugly person."

"Wow! Like you never thought that someone thought of you that way or you didn't know this many good things about yourself." "Oh goodness. I love validations. You may not think telling someone positive things is fun, but you feel so good after you have made them smile."

"Some people who get picked on get told what is great about them." "When I was feeling down, the validation really helped. It makes me stronger as a person."

Appendix B

Sample Validation Letter to Parents

Dear Parents:

Every school commits itself to finding a variety of ways to uphold, acknowledge, and reinforce two important goals:

1. Academic achievement
2. Responsible citizenship

It is my pleasure to let you know that the _____ grade(s) will soon begin a "Validation Program" as a supplement to our reading, writing, listening, speaking, and character education programs. We have learned that the Validation Program helps reinforce and promote academic achievement and responsible citizenship.

What is validation? Once a week, your child will write a validation about one of the other students or adults in his or her _____class. After validations are written, students will share them in front of the class during the weekly Validation Time. (Validation will take place on Fridays during _____.)

Students know there are only two rules to follow when writing validations:

- First, everything written about their validation partner must be *true*.

- Second, everything written must be *good* (positive).

How does validation work? Each week, your child will be paired with a different student (or adult) in the class, thus becoming validation partners for that week. (The teacher also becomes a weekly validation partner with one of the students.) Everyone writes a validation about his or her partner. Generally, your child prepares his or her validation at home where he or she may spend time concentrating and writing. Your child will know who his or her partner will be early in the week and will have the week to prepare the validation. It is important for students to remember to bring their validations to school for Validation Time.

After all students finish sharing validations, the teacher conducts a teaching session with the class. During this session, the teacher highlights important information gleaned from validations. This Synthesis Session reinforces the academic successes and exemplary responsible citizenship comments identified during Validation Time that day. The teacher also uses the comments from validations to reinforce school and classroom expectations about learning and behaving responsibly.

Students of all ages have found the Validation Program to be successful for many reasons. First, your child receives direct, positive information about himself or herself. Because everyone in the class hears the successful attributes about each other, students are motivated toward continuous improvement. Their writing, reading, speaking, and listening skills develop and flourish with this experience. Students become increasingly comfortable standing before the class and more positive in their attitudes and perceptions about others.

As your child receives more and more validations throughout the year, you will find he or she will become more appreciative and proud of his or her validations. Be sure to take a look at them as they come home.

We are happy to begin validation, not only as a program that improves communication skills, but also because it is a powerful and positive influence in the lives of our students. If you have any questions, please feel free to contact your child's teacher, _____ and/or _____.

Sincerely,

(Note: This letter is a simple example of the parent letter you might want to write to the parents in your community. You will certainly decide the total content you wish to include.)

Appendix C

Suggested Lesson Plan for Introducing the Validation Program

The Validation Process is really good. It makes you feel better after someone has validated you. It's a bit embarrassing at first, but after a while it isn't that hard to stand in front of your classmates. It's worth its weight in gold.

— Seventh-grade student

Begin with an explanation that everyone in the class is doing the "Val" Program. You will need to let students know no one is exempt from being a partner to another (unless there is a student with special exceptions). Each has the unique opportunity to launch the program!

1. Talk about what the program is: a written validation of each partner each week. Partners will change each week and they may be paired with other students, the teacher, or other adults.

2. Discuss the only two guidelines: everything they write must be *good* and *true*.

3. Define what *good* and *true* mean. Each validation must be 100 percent good and 100 percent true.

4. Validations are to be written at home, in their own domain or private area. Partners will be assigned one week ahead of time and are due the following Friday (or whatever day the school or teacher decides.) Later in the program, you might want to guide or nudge students to consider different forms/kinds/styles of writing as they prepare their written validations.

5. Students bring the validation to school and put them in their validation folders—folders that will remain in a designated location in the classroom—until Validation Time. (You, the teacher, can decide how to go about this and where their val folders are to be kept.)

6. Explain that after they have written their validations, they will come to the front of the room to read them aloud to their partner. Let them know the partner whose name is called first will be the person who is to read first. When they are finished reading, they give the written validation to their partners. (Note: it is important to assure students that if they feel anxious or nervous at first, that's okay, because almost everyone will be a little nervous reading their validations at first.)

7. Then remind everyone that when partners are reading their validations to their partner, they—as audience members—get the luxury of being able to hear all the good things everyone has to say about each other. Discuss your expectations for behavior, especially

listening politely and openly at this time. Disruptions, disrespect, etc., are not acceptable and will not be excused.

8. Next, select two potential partners to come to the front of the room and model the acceptable way of reading validations to each other (standing three to five feet apart). At this point, to model the procedures step by step, you will want to "call out" each step of the procedure: students are to stand face-to-face, looking only at each other directly and soaking up all the good things they hear. After the first validation partner pretends to read a blank val, he or she puts his or her validation behind his or her back, and then the next partner takes out his or her validation from behind his or her back. After both have pretended to read blank validations, they exchange them and kindly "acknowledge" the receipt of the validation (e.g., saying "thank you," shaking hands, etc.).

9. While modeling the procedures you first coached students through, you might want to imprint this process upon their brains by asking two other students to come to the front of the room to do the same procedures. At the same time, call another two students to come and stand by these two students to monitor and "coach" the first two students through each step of the process. You might even want to try having a third set of students to come up front and do the same thing—except this time silently go through the process without anyone coaching them through each procedure. Ask everyone in the class to watch closely to see if the last group goes through the process correctly.

10. We've also learned that it is best to tell and show students how they are to walk back to their seats quietly, softly, and respectfully after receiving their validations.

11. Beware the pitfalls—share the seven pitfalls with the class and explain each thoroughly:
    a. forgetting
    b. "Oh no! Not a (boy or girl)"
    c. "Oh no! I don't like _____"
    d. avoiding texting, Tweeting, Facebooking, etc., in advance
    e. bestowing unnecessary, inappropriate gifts, toys, or other goodies
    f. being tempted to go beyond giving purely honest comments
    g. use of first-person singular pronouns when writing and reading one's validation—use "you" rather than "I, he, or she"

12. The teacher then explains that when students get back to their desks, they are to place their validations in their validation folders.

13. Lastly, tell students when they can take their validations home. (You can talk about this at your class/team/faculty meetings and then you can share it with your students.)

14. **Other items:**
    At some point, you may want to share with students the importance of listening, including Ralph Nichols's list of the worst listening habits. As mentioned earlier in the text, you can access the websites: http://listeningleaders.com/home.html and http://www.listen.org.

    You will want to mention that a signed letter explaining the Validation Program may come from the principal, the whole administration team, or you. It will then be sent to the parents either through e-mail, regular mail, or with the students when they go home.

    Do not hesitate to ask the principal, assistant principal, curriculum coordinator (or whoever the trainer or curriculum coordinator happens to be who introduced the Validation Program) if you have questions/concerns or need assistance. Consider pairing and validating each other at your class/team/faculty meetings each week to share validations.

- Consider pairing and validating each other at your class/team/faculty meetings each week to share validations.

- Consider pairing the administrators, guidance counselor(s), and other instructional and noninstructional personnel with your students each week. The more you involve as many school personnel as possible in validation, the more successful the program will be for the entire school. (Consider including secretaries, aids, security personnel, assistants, food service personnel, custodians, school bus drivers, etc., and do so every week.)

The success/failure of this program hinges on your sincere dedication and commitment to it. It has pronounced potential to benefit and empower our entire school community, but it's going to take some time and a great deal of effort. Thank you for being willing to take a chance on something new that has proven to make a huge impact on students' personal development, character, emotional intelligence, general goodwill toward all, and exemplary positive school climate and culture. Next year, you might want to let your students know that your classroom and others within the school will be participating in the Validation Program.

Appendix D

Other Considerations for Teachers to Build Upon and Reinforce the Validation Notion

Three Major Issues to Keep in Mind

A. Validation is not just an add-on curriculum. It is a component of a virtues-based school helping students become other-oriented and positive instead of looking through the lenses of "me-ness." It is also a perfect opportunity for school personnel to make a difference by leading with integrity and creating a positive school and classroom climate.

B. Validation permits students to observe, identify, and reinforce character traits modeled by all educators, staff, and other students. It is an effective way for students to learn about character by truly seeing it "in action" and applying it to real-life situations.

C. Sharing the positive traits students see in each other is "putting into action" what defines and establishes a qualitative school culture. Seeing, defining, and living the positive traits and values of life is a major key to success.

Supplemental Supportive Approaches:

1. Add to and/or remind students of your current school's mission statement as an important school-wide document underlying and embracing the essential virtues of good character. Consider adopting your own classroom's mission statement, maybe even something to the effect of, "Our Team: It's not about Me. It's about Us."

2. Introduce various virtues that are represented in certain notable children's literature stories or other book extracts by reading them aloud to your students. It has been found that reading aloud to middle and high school students some children's lit books has had surprisingly positive results. Reading these at the beginning of Validation Time, or at the end, provides positive reminders that help students understand and explore the values/virtues and examples thereof. Some book examples: *Love You Forever* by Robert Munsch, *The Wednesday Surprise* by Eve Bunting, *Doodle Flute* by Daniel Pinkwater, and *The Knee Baby* by Mary Jarrell and spectacularly illustrated by Symeon Shimin.

3. Begin to think about how you could go about designing mini-lessons or have classroom discussions exploring one or two specific examples and behaviors of the values/virtues of life. Do so before or after Validation Time, or any other time. This could also be done during the Synthesis Session.

4. Display posters, signs, charts, note cards, etc., of various virtues. (See www.characterfirst .com for sample virtue cards, along with other virtues websites mentioned.)

5. Call attention to (and/or ask students) which teachers, staff, administrators, historical figures, etc., model the specific values, virtues, and behaviors we all want to see. Ask them to define these virtues.

6. Find, identify, and occasionally share various songs that illustrate some of the virtues to reinforce. Play all of or sections of the song at the beginning of Validation Time (e.g., Aretha Franklin's "Respect"; the Beatles' "All You Need Is Love"; War's "Why Can't We Be Friends?"; the Eagles' "Peaceful Easy Feeling"; and the Eagles' "There's a Hole in the World Tonight").

7. Select some short clips from films, videos, etc., that reflect examples of good character traits and virtues. Play a clip before or after validation as discussion points for greater understanding and awareness. (See "Film Clips for Character Education" at www.flimclipsonline.com for eighty-nine clips. Also examine "Superheroes" resources at www.healthyheroes.com for board games, interactive website, comic books, and other activities that illustrate superheroes' minds and hearts leading students in positive directions.)

8. Search and review various professional resources that will joyfully enhance your background knowledge of virtues and sound character development. Visit the Journal of Research in Character Education (www.infoagepub.com). The Character Education Partnership (CEP) offers Eleven Principles of Effective Character Education (www.character.com). "Got Character," a character newsletter written for staff and parents providing definitions and examples of the various virtues and character traits you might want to use can be found at www.lindbergschools.ws. Institute for Excellence & Ethics provides curriculum resources, toolkits, and assessments at www.excellenceandethics.org.

9. Review and consider incorporating the eleven Character Education Partnership (CEP) principles as part of an interdisciplinary character education approach in the various overall curriculum courses within the school. These principles call on schools to address character education in the overall school climate, in extracurricular activities, and in various school committees.

10. Establish a type of validation "committee" or "team" made up of faculty, administrators, counselors, the School Resource Officer, the Parent Teacher Organization, other school personnel, parents, and students to review, support, and provide guidance and assistance to enhance the success and growth of the program. Use an acronym like the VCRSG (Validation Committee to Review, Support, and Guide)—or any other acronym or combination of letters for its name that you prefer.

11. Additionally, consider creating and establishing a student organized and operated "character council" to look at issues that come up and to improve the program. Years ago, alongside the Validation Program we also set up a "Pos Squad," (Positive Squad), a group of seven students who remained unknown, like the Secret Seven Society at the University of Virginia. These students remain anonymous but independently send little Pos Squad notes to individuals about a particular good deed witnessed.

12. Implement a research-based survey as a needs assessment and springboard for addressing areas of improvement and documentation of outcomes. (The National School Climate Center [NSCC] uses "The Comprehensive School Climate Inventory" at www.schoolclimate.org/climate/practice.php.)

Other sources to consider:

www.emc.cmich.edu/CharacterEd/assessments.htm

http://www.goodcharacter.com/assessment.html

Also consider using student and teacher questionnaires about the program's progress, success, and impact through this type of qualitative survey instrument.

The eleventh principle spelled out by the Character Education Partnership professional organization states, "The school regularly assesses its culture and climate, the functioning of its staff as character educators, and the extent to which its students manifest good character."

13. Remind each other that educators are key leaders—and indeed "significant others"—who are major influences in all students' lives. As we connect and build positive relationships with students, we are role-model examples of what it means to be a good human being and effective educator. You are an ethical role model for them. When you can reach them, you know you can really teach them. Plus, reinforce the notion that in your classroom they are to realize that they will experience being in "good company" as identified in Frank Smith's "The History of Education in Seven Words: You Learn from the Company You Keep."

14. Remind students they are in a "team" classroom, a "Golden Rule" classroom. Educators consciously or unconsciously "teach" what they "accept." When students know we are committed to using kind, affirming words in the classroom, when they know "rudeness is out the door," they know what's accepted and what isn't.

15. One last suggestion. You might want to pursue another possibility—a "tables turned" adventure. Consider asking your students to come up with a list of things they don't want to see or hear in the classroom. This kind of opportunity gives them ownership for helping to define and create a positive classroom climate. Consider crafting their comments onto a poster (or list) of what your classroom is all about. Validation is easily accepted in such a climate. The neurolinguistic nourishing language that occurs is more likely to become automatically engrained in the mind, and in their behavior.

We all know that proper implementation is crucial to the success of any new program. With that in mind, you can use the above "lesson plan" as you introduce validation to your students this week. You may need twenty to thirty minutes, and after sharing all the essential information about the program, you will want to model an appropriate validation as well. (This approach will show students how validations are orally shared. You might pair yourself with another adult, teacher, or even one of the students and model how the program unfolds.) This should be done before you assign your first set of partners. Afterward you can announce when the first round of validation presentations will take place and announce partner pairings.

Appendix E

Effective and Ineffective Acknowledgment

In an effort to assist us in making our acknowledgments of others effective and specific, below is some of Jerry Brophy's (Brophy, 1981) list of effective and ineffective comments which initially were compiled under the title of "effective praise" and "ineffective praise." For reasons listed earlier, the lists are simply reworded as "effective acknowledgment" and "ineffective acknowledgment."

Effective Acknowledgment

- is focused and given in recognition of noteworthy effort.
- specifies the particulars of one's efforts and resulting accomplishments.
- is delivered conversationally and with sincere credibility.
- acknowledges attainment of specified performance criteria.
- provides information to students about their competence or the value of their accomplishments.
- orients students toward appreciation of their own task-related behavior and thinking.
- uses students' prior accomplishments as a context for describing present accomplishments.
- attributes success to effort and ability, implying that similar successes can be expected in the future.
- focuses students' attention on their own task-relevant behavior.

Ineffective Acknowledgment

- is delivered randomly, unsystematically or with superficial exaggeration.
- is restricted to global positive reactions.
- shows a bland uniformity, suggesting a conditioned response made with minimal attention.
- rewards mere participation, without regard to the effort expended or the meaning of the accomplishment.
- provides little information at all or gives students inflated information about their status.
- orients students toward comparing themselves with others and thinking about competing.

- uses the accomplishments of peers as the context for describing students' present accomplishments.

- attributes success to external factors, such as luck, or easy task, or to please the teacher.

- focuses students' attention on the teacher as an external authority figure who is manipulating them.

Appendix F

Pairing Adult Partners at Staff Meetings/Workshops/Training Sessions

When validation is first introduced at staff meetings, or at initial workshops/training sessions, we've found it effective to ask those attending to prepare a validation for one of their colleagues who are at the session. Later they present their validations as part of the direct participatory involvement in the workshop. However, with as many as thirty possible attendees, time may be a factor for everyone to write a validation. One option would be to break the group into two, three, or four groups, with someone designated as the moderator-coordinator for each group.

In the past, some schools have decided to share their first validations at the next faculty meeting or at another scheduled time. Central office personnel have actually woven validations into the beginning of their monthly or semi-monthly meetings. Individual schools have also decided to do validations at faculty meetings, involving the teachers, administrators, and staff members.

One approach toward beginning the first validation session would be to simply write each person's name on a slip of paper and draw them out of a hat. After validations are written, you could ask for volunteers to come forward and read their validations. That approach has worked well. There are always three or more partners who are ready and eager to share their validations with everyone in the group.

Another approach is to pre-pair partners, based upon the suggestion we give to teachers who are going to implement the program in their classrooms. The suggestion is to "pre-pair for success." In the classroom, especially when beginning the first session of validation, it is important initially for teachers to pair each student with another student the teacher knows will very likely be a successful match.

The point is to begin successfully by ensuring that those who are paired will be comfortable with each other, if not eager and happy about being paired together. This way, everyone will more likely begin the validation experience comfortably and positively, viewing the experience as interesting, if not nifty and enjoyable. Pairing partners this way will likely insure the Validation Program will begin positively and successfully.

Appendix G

Institute of Educational Sciences (ies) National Center for Education Statistics Website

http://nces.ed.gov/programs/crimeindicators/crimeindicators2011/key.asp

The source of this information comes from the US Department of Education, Institute of Education Sciences, National Center for Education Statistics, US Department of Education.

Without listing the huge numbers of data available in the above website, the examples below represent only about 4 percent of the total data listed on the website.

Indicators of School Crime and Safety: February 2012

Preliminary data show there were thirty-three school-associated violent deaths from July 1, 2009, through June 30, 2010. (In the school year 2008–09, there were thirty-eight violent deaths among students ages five to eighteen.)

In 2010, among students ages twelve to eighteen, there were about 828,000 nonfatal victimizations at school, which includes 470,000 victims of theft, and 359,000 victims of violence (simple assault and serious violence). In 2009–10, about 74 percent of public schools recorded one or more violent incidents of crime, 16 percent recorded one or more serious violent incidents, and 44 percent recorded one or more thefts.

Violent Deaths

- During the school year 2008–09 there were 1,579 homicides among school-age youth ages five to eighteen, of which seventeen occurred at school. During the 2008 calendar year, there were 1,344 suicides of youth ages five to eighteen, of which seven occurred at school.

Nonfatal Student and Teacher Victimization

- In 2010, students ages twelve to eighteen were victims of about 828,000 nonfatal victimizations at school, including 470,000 thefts and 359,000 violent victimizations, 91,400 of which were serious violent victimizations.

- In 2009, about 10 percent of male students in grades 9–12 reported being threatened or injured with a weapon on school property in the past year, compared to 5 percent of female students.

School Environment

- During the 2009–10 school year, 85 percent of public schools recorded that one or more crime incidents had taken place at school, amounting to an estimated 1.9 million crimes. This figure translates to a rate of forty crimes per 1,000 public school students enrolled in 2009–10.

Fights, Weapons, and Illegal Substances

- In 2009, about 31 percent of students in grades 9–12 reported they had been in a physical fight at least one time during the previous twelve months in various locations.
- In 2009, about 27 percent of males carried a weapon anywhere, compared to 7 percent of females, and 8 percent of males carried a weapon on school property, compared to 3 percent of females.

National Center for Education Statistics: http://nces.ed.gov.

The shortest and surest way to live with honor in the world is to be in reality what we would appear to be; all human virtues increase and strengthen themselves by the practice and experience of them.

—Socrates

Appendix H

Additional Written Testimonies
of the Validation Program

The first document below was typed and sent to me by a mother (also a teacher who had not implemented the program) on March 6, 1989.

1. "My seven-year-old son bought a card while we were shopping, and I asked him what he intended to do with the card. It had pictures of cats on the front, which he dearly loves. This was in October, and he said, 'Mom, I want to validate you for Mother's Day, that's why I got this card.' He did the validation and put it in his blue treasure box to keep for nine months until this May. Validations have become a way of life for me and my family, not only in my classroom but also at home."

The next document is by Ms. Mondrey, an assistant principal of a middle school in 2012.

2. "Words cannot accurately express how validation makes you feel, but it has made my day on more than one occasion! I may be having the most stressful, horrible, exhausting day and then I receive a validation from a student and that all goes away and I find myself re-energized.

"Why? One, the look on the student's face as you read his/her validation is priceless. That student feels valued, special, important… and everyone else is hearing what you are saying about him/her. Two, it's truly fascinating what students notice about you and what about you is important to them. Three, that student has taken the time to get to know you, put in the effort to write it down, and worked up the courage to say it face to face in front of others. The Validation Program teaches students to look for the good in others—to recognize, acknowledge, and appreciate it—regardless of how they feel about that person. What more valuable tool could we give them?

"I was first exposed to the Validation Program several years ago in Dr. Pirkle's graduate classes. He would have us validate each other as part of the process of becoming educational leaders. I then tried out the program with my own students; however, as a teacher, I never had the administrative support needed to fully implement this program with my students.

Fast forward a few years … I was working as an Assistant Principal at Louisa Middle School (my current position). The 8th grade teachers and I were looking for ways to reach our group of 'challenging' students—they were mean to each other, superficial, and full of hateful drama (more so than your 'normal' middle-schoolers). Discouraged and disheartened, we were emotionally drained by October that year. In talking with my friend and colleague, Jenn Purcell (8th grade guidance counselor), I mentioned the Validation Program. She immediately responded to the concept, so we pitched it to the teachers. They wanted to give it a shot, so we talked to the principal and brought Dr. Pirkle in for training. We started doing validations with approximately 380 students (the whole 8th grade class) in January and continued every Friday for the remainder of the school year. By March, there was a noticeable change in our students—they were more accepting of each other, more willing to compromise, more compassionate towards those who were different from them, and more positive overall. The program worked so well, we trained the rest of the faculty and implemented the program school-wide the following year. At the teachers' request, we even started doing faculty validations at our monthly meetings!

"It may be difficult to grasp how such a simple program can have such a profound impact, yet it does. Perhaps it is precisely *because* it is so "simple" in principle—basically, recognize what's good about someone else and tell that person—that it works so well. I mean, how often do any of us hear the *good*? Usually, it's what we've done wrong, what we could do better, or how we're not good enough. But, it's not easy. It takes commitment on the part of all involved: students, teachers, parents, and administration. And it must be modeled, monitored, facilitated, and guided by caring adults in order for it to succeed. The effect is not immediately noticeable. In fact, the true impact cannot be measured and may not be realized for many years. (Just as you may not realize the impact a good teacher has had on your life until many years later.) However, it is absolutely there.

"The Validation Program is, without doubt, the most important and meaningful thing I've ever been involved in!"

The next sample comes from Greg Palmer, eighth-grade math teacher, 2012

3. "The first year the Validation Program came to our middle school, I had a very difficult group of students in my third-period class. What I observed with this group is that the female students did not get along well for a host of reasons. One noticeable area of contention was differing socioeconomic backgrounds. The girls from higher socioeconomic situations felt they were better that their less fortunate peers. One young lady told me something to the effect, 'I would never be friends with that trash. Do you see the way she is dressed? Her clothes look like she bought them at the Goodwill.' Additionally, there was some racial tension in the room; this tension existed between both genders. For the most part, the issues between the boys revolved around competition for attention from the girls.

"The validations started off slow, and with some resistance, but I don't think I have ever witnessed this type of growth in maturity in a group of students in such a short period of time. In today's modern, secular world, we spend very little time transmitting values to our youth. A society without values is bankrupt. The Validation Program is one way to transmit these badly needed values to our youth."

The last example is a document sent in August 2012 by an eighth-grade math teacher and assistant football coach.

4. "As an eighth-grade teacher for the last two years I have been given the opportunity to be involved with the Validation Program with two very different groups of young people. My first group of students was more open to the program and willing to give it a chance because my class was a very close group. Each student in that first class seemed to be friends with pretty much everyone else, where the class I had this last year was more segregated into different friend groups.

"The first thing that stands out to me as a teacher is that the students and adults who put time and effort into their validations definitely get more out of the program than those who tend to do the minimum. Throughout the year, I saw a couple of students who did not seem to have many friends in my class really start to open up and express themselves more and more as the year went on. These students were not used to hearing their peers say nice things about them and became more excited and open as we went through the Validation Program.

"One student who comes to mind from this past year always kept to himself at all times even when given an opportunity to work with a partner or small group in class. This student always said he felt more comfortable working alone. In my opinion, with the help of the Validation Program and hearing other peers and adults finally recognize the good in him, this student began to open up, participate more in class discussions, and really find a small group of students he could build friendships with for quite possibly the first time.

"The transformations that can occur with some students are really awesome to see and go through with the students. As a teacher being involved with the students every single day in the classroom, you build the typical student–teacher relationship, but this allows the teacher to get to know the students in a different way. Each day we get to see the students perform in our classroom, but this allows us to develop a better understanding of the students in a different light. You are able to see the interests, talents, and abilities that each student possesses outside of solving the multistep equation or finding the slope of a line given two points for example. At the same time it allows the students to get to know their teacher outside of the guy always pushing us to get our work done or working quietly on an assignment.

"The program definitely enables the teacher and students to truly get to know and understand one another while at the same time being encouraged and uplifted for the good in each of them. The Validation Program is really a two-part program when it is done correctly. The first part is having someone validate you for the good that exists inside you, but the second part is allowing you the opportunity to truly look at another person, strip away everything the world sees, and genuinely get to know the good that exists in your partner. No matter whether you are being validated or doing the validating, you will find out that either way, you are being rewarded."

Appendix I

Additional Empathy Information Websites

Additional Empathy informational websites:

Key Information on the Roots of Empathy: http://www.rootsofempathy.org/keyinformation
.html.

Empathy: http://eqi.org/empathy.htm.

Empathy and Its Relationship with Listening, Trust, and Defusing Conflicts: http://www
.businessballs.com/empathy.htm.

Empathy and Morality: http://www.agnosticmom.com/2007/03/25/much-of-our-morality-lies-
in-the-brain.

Overview of Empathy: http://xnet.kp.org/permanentejournal/fall03/cpc.html.

Appendix J

Samples of Actual Validations Written by Student to Principal, Teacher to Student, Father to Daughter, and Wife to Husband

* Mrs. Horn *

I am so glad you are my principal. You are very supportive of all of the students in our school. You are also extremely hard working and dependable. If I ever needed your help I know you would be there. You always seem to have a positive attitude and that makes you fun to be around. Mrs. Horn you are so enjoyable and I am glad you are my principal!!

FROM: ALEX Bishop

Ms. Ginders class

Student-to-Principal Validation

RECIPE FOR A NUMBER ONE NIKKI

Take at least a 3.0 average portion of SCHOLARSHIP.
Stir in plenty of CITIZENSHIP verified by pleased teachers.
Spice up with PARTICIPATION in extra-curricular activities.
Store far away from U's in conduct.
Simmer with hope for joining National Junior Honor Society.

Dear Nikki,

You are diligent, cheerful, reliable, thoughtful, fun-loving, and polite. You are always willing to help others, and you are good at cheering others on toward being their best. Your eager attitude and lovely smile warm and encourage me each morning. You earn the respect of students and teachers alike with your hard work, pleasant personality, and sterling character. As you stay true to yourself, the world will be a better place.

Love,
Mrs. Hoag

Teacher-to-Student Validation

22 Feb 88

Dear Dana

It is a real pleasure to be your validation father. As a matter of fact, this is the most pleasant thing I've done all month.

You are better than any little girl I know for many reasons. You are always happy. Being cheerful and happy is the best way to approach life. There is an old saying that says; 'Smile and the world smiles with you, frown and you frown alone.' Your smile makes me happy and feel great.

Besides being as cheerful as a sunny spring day, you are cuter than a speckled pup. I had a speckled pup once. His name was Buster. He was a fantastic looking dog, — but your better looking than Buster with a new collar and a bow in his hair. Actually, you are more than cute. You are a beautiful girl.

Beauty, although it's nice, isn't the most important thing. I'd rather have a friend who was kind and considerate than beautiful. You are very kind and considerate. People who are really bright have learned that being kind and thoughtful is much more important than outward beauty. Did you know it is possible to be beautiful inside? You are.

I've enjoyed this because I like to think about nice people. You one of the nicest people I know.

I love you!
Dad

Father-to-Daughter Validation

April 29, 2007

Dear Butch,

I wonder if you had any idea two years ago how well acquainted you and Campbell's Soup were going to become? Or that your primary job qualifications for any future resumes were going to be "Chief Cook, bottle washer, proofreader and laundry folder-er?" How do I say "thank you" for all you have put up with while I do this graduate thing? While I have tried to be the "mom" for all the things the kids needed to have, I certainly have not always been the "wife." Thank goodness you are able to sleep through all those late nights of me pecking away on the computer. Thank goodness you didn't seem to mind when I said, once again, "Honey, do you mind if...." or "Hey, can you do this one thing for me?"

There is no way that I could have pursued this course of study without your support. Not once have you complained when I chose to outline a chapter rather than vacuum the floor. You don't even complain when you have to listen to me go on and on about OFSs, computer glitches, and internship proposals. You have been the epitome of patience and encouragement, and I am sure, have put your own plans and needs second to mine more times than I am willing to admit.

I appreciate more than I can put into words the fact that you have let me take you for granted, and I know I have abused that privilege far more than you deserve. If and when I complete this program, it will certainly not be a degree that I have earned, but one that the two of us have earned together. If I didn't think Longwood would charge double for it, I would request both our names on the diploma!

Other husbands made of far less quality "stuff" would have never sacrificed as you have for me to get through these classes. I am so thankful that I chose to go on life's journey with you all those years ago, and even more thankful that you asked me! What an example you have been to our children. Both of them will have a true picture of what a man is supposed to be because of the model you have set for them. I am so glad to have you as my best friend.

Love,
K

Wife-to-Husband Validation

Appendix K

Sample Chart for Scheduling and Tracking the Pairings of Student Partners

This first sample chart (titled Figure 1) is partially filled-in with the first two weeks of pairings that are recorded. The following chart is the same, except it is mostly filled-in. You may be able to create another type of pairing chart or record of pairings that is more functional for you.

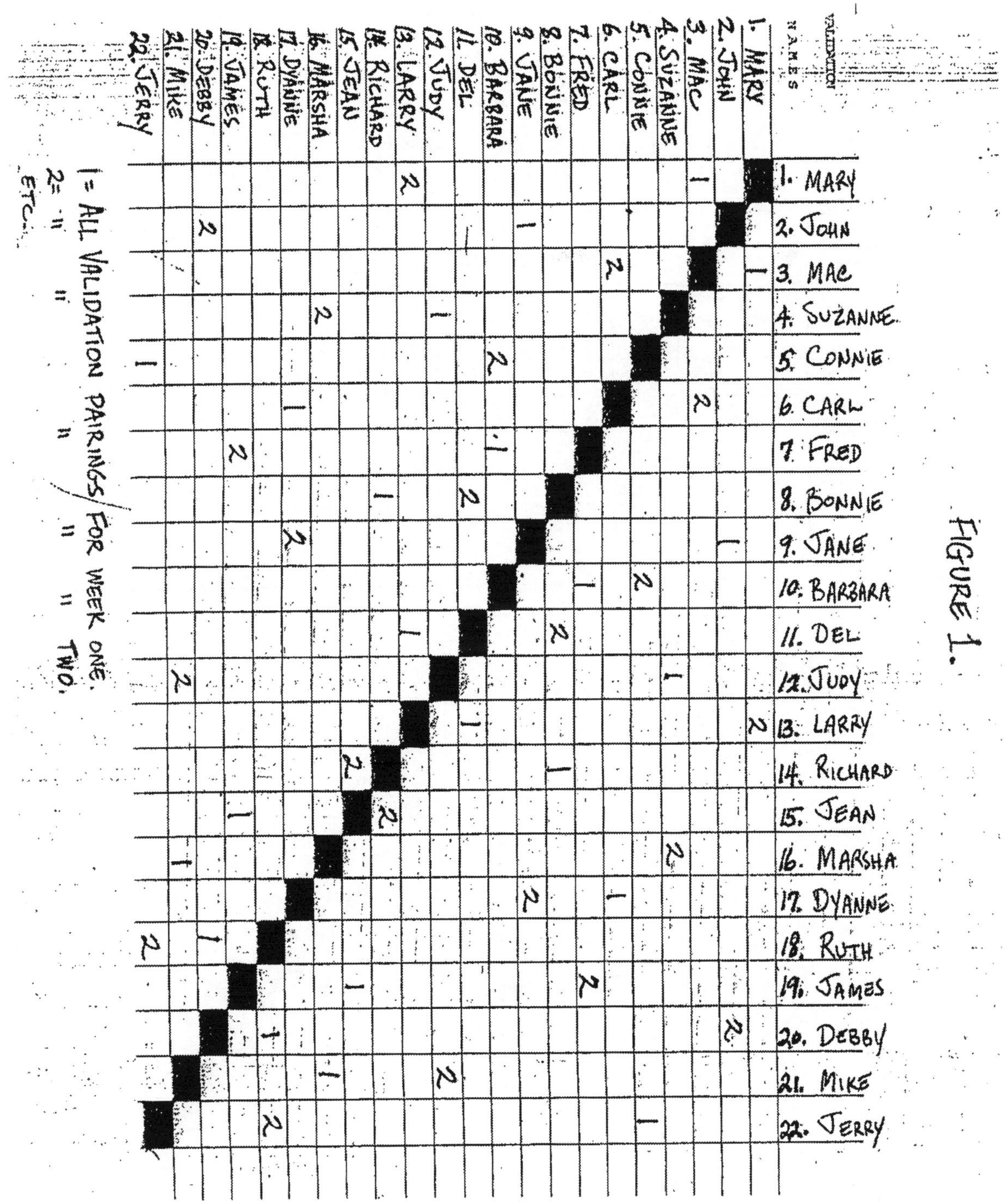
FIGURE 1.
NAMES
1. MARY
2. JOHN
3. MAC
4. SUZANNE
5. CONNIE
6. CARL
7. FRED
8. BONNIE
9. JANE
10. BARBARA
11. DEL
12. JUDY
13. LARRY
14. RICHARD
15. JEAN
16. MARSHA
17. DYANNE
18. RUTH
19. JAMES
20. DEBBY
21. MIKE
22. JERRY
1 = ALL VALIDATION PAIRINGS FOR WEEK ONE.
2= " " " " TWO.
ETC.

Figure 1

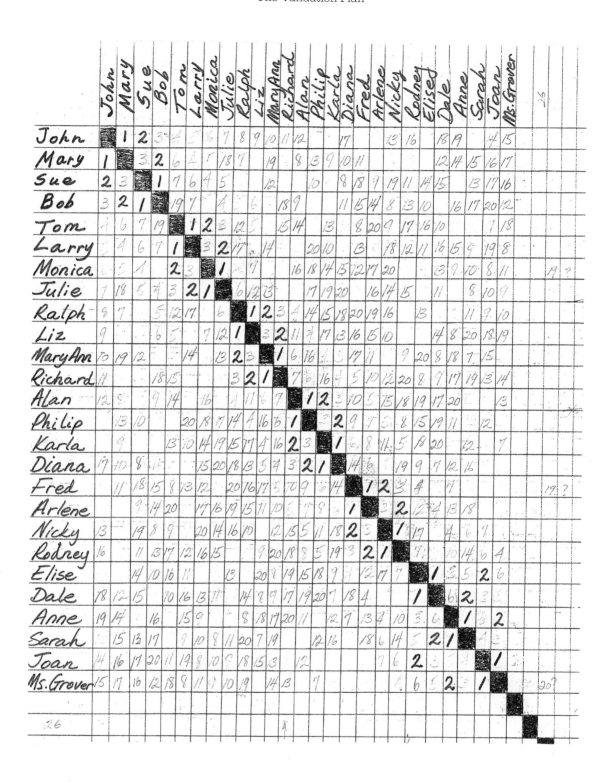

Figure 2

70

Appendix L

Document for Reflection

This document reflects a single assessment example (form) one school used for assessing the Validation Program after a semester of implementation. This document reflects a single assessment example (form) one school used for assessing the Validation Program after a semester of implementation.

Judith Osser
5/6 French
— 1988 —
US, UK, Canadian
Students

Faculty/Staff Evaluation

(Please circle one)

HOW MUCH HAS VALIDATION HELPED STUDENTS:	1 No Help	2 Some Help	3 Much Help
1. read/speak in front of others?	1	2	(3)
2. writing skills?	1	2	(3)
3. listening skills?	1	2	(3)
4. self-esteem?	1	2	(3)
5. look for positive traits in others?	1	2	(3)
6. develop an "other-oriented," less egocentric attitude toward others?	1	2	(3)
7. be more coorperative toward one another?	1	2	(3)

(Please place an x on the continuum)

8. How honest are others' Validations?

Not honest |___|___|___X___| Very honest

9. How do you like Validation?

Not so swell |___|___|___XXX—| Very much

10. What immediate carryover behaviors has Validation evoked for your students?

_ THEY ARE LIVING UP TO THE POSITIVE STATEMENTS MADE BY OTHERS.
_ THEY DO NOT "GET ON EACH OTHERS' CASE" AS MUCH.
- THEY ARE MORE SPONTANEOUSLY APPRECIATIVE AND FORGIVING.

11. What are Validations' strengths?

MANY STUDENTS HAVE, ON THEIR OWN, EXPLORED DIFFERENT "LITERARY" FORMS. THEY HAVE LEARNED TO DESCRIBE USING MANY EXPRESSIVE ADJECTIVES. THEY HAVE BEEN LEARNING, BY DOING THE SYNTHESIS, TO EVALUATE OTHERS IN A CONSTRUCTIVE AND ENCOURAGING MANNER.

12. What are Validations' weaknesses?

CAN'T THINK OF ANY.

Bibliography

Alliance for Excellent Education. "High School Dropouts in America." Fact Sheet. September 2010. www.all4ed.org.

Begley, Sharon. "31 Ways To Get Smarter in 2012." *Newsweek* (January 9, 2012): 35.

Bradshaw, John. *Reclaiming Virtue*. New York: Random House, 2009.

Brooks, David. *The Social Animal, the Source of Love, Character, and Achievement*. New York: Random House, 2012.

Brophy, Jerry. "Teacher Praise: A Functional Analysis." *Review of Educational Research* 51 (1981): 5–32.

Brown, Harriet. "The Boom and Bust Ego." *Psychology Today* (February 2012): 66–70.

CEP, Character Education Partnership. "Key Topics" link to "Performance Values." DC. June 10, 2010. www.character.org.

Coles, Robert. *The Moral Intelligence of Children*. New York: Random House, 1997.

Covey, Stephen. *The Seven Habits of Highly Effective People*. New York: Simon and Schuster, 1988.

Dewey, John. *Experience and Education*. New York: Collier, 1938.

Dokoupil, Tony. "Tweets, Texts, E-mail, Posts: Is the Onslaught Making Us Crazy?" *Psychology Today* (June 12, 2012): 24–36.

Educational Leadership SuperSite. "Interstate School Leaders Licensure Consortium Standards for School Leaders." 2006. http://wps.ablongman.com/ab_bacon_edadmin_1/0,6183,462533-,00 .html.

Edwards, Jenny. *Inviting Students to Learn: 100 Tips for Talking Effectively with Your Students*. ASCD. Alexandria, Virginia. http://www.ascd.org/publications/books/110015.aspx.

Goleman, Daniel. *Emotional Intelligence*. New York: Bantam Books, 1995.

Haynes, Charles C. "Schools of Conscience." *Educational Leadership* (May 2009): 6–13.

Hultberg, Nelson. "Restoring the Eternal Verities." May 14, 2004. http://www.afr.org/ Hultberg/051404.html.

International Listening Leadership Institute. "Listening Leaders Honor Giants." November 9, 2005. http://casts.webvalence.com/sites/ListeningLeader/Broadcast.D20051109.html.

International Listening Association. "Listening Lesson Interviews." Summer 2003. V. 84. http://www.listen.org/Legend.

Jackson, Sharon. "Ever-Present Devices Can Push Our Crazy Buttons." *USA Today* (March 27, 2012): 1D.

Kaufman, Scott Berry. "How to Spot a Narcissist." *Psychology Today* (July 5, 2011).

Lewis, Al. "Dead by 50? Thank You!" *Wall Street Journal Sunday* (January 13, 2013).

Marcus, Mary Brophy. "What Would Cause a Young Person to Snap?" *USA Today* (January 10, 2010): 4D.

Nass, Clifford. "Are We Losing Empathy?" *USA Today* (October 20, 2010): 9A.

Nichols, Ralph, and Leonard Stevens. "Listening to People." *Harvard Business Review* (1957–99): 1–6.

Nichols, Ralph. "Listening Is a 10 Part Skill." (1954) International Listening Association. Belle Plaine, MN. http://www.listen.org/Nichols10Partspeech. Click on Part A and Part B. An additional "Listening" informational website: http://www.listen.org/Legend.

SCAN, Organization Newsletter. *Style Weekly*. March 12, 2011. Richmond, VA.

Scherer, Marge. "Finessing Feedback." *ASCD Educational Leadership* 70, no. 1 (Sept. 2012): 7. http://www.ascd.org/publications/educational leader-ship/sept12/vol70/num01/Finessing-Feedback.aspx.

Statistics Brain. "High School Dropout Statistics." 12 Oct, 2012. Education Week, Children Trends Database. http://www.statisticbrain.com/high-school-dropout-statistics/.

Stern, Robin. "Social and Emotional Learning." www.education.com. Nov. 2012. http://www.education.com/reference/article/Ref_Social_Learning_What/.

Stillwell, Charles. "Building Leadership through Collaboration." *Richmond Times-Dispatch* (November 17, 2011): A9.

Stop Cyberbullying. 2012. http://www.stopcyberbullying.org/parents/youth_empowered_solutions.html.

Svoboda, Elizabeth. "Lessons for Living." *Psychology Today* (September/October 2012): 60.

Szabo, Liz. "Violence 'Ages' Children's DNA." *USA Today* (April 24, 2012): 1.

The Week. "Battling Bullies." (November 12, 2010): 15.

———. "Creating a 'Mind Meld' by Talking." (August 10, 2010).

About the Author

As a child growing up in Chattanooga, Tennessee, James Pirkle lived in the Veteran's Projects for the majority of his childhood. One day in his senior year during a history class, the class was discussing the new law that would do away with segregated schools. He spoke in favor of the law to the overwhelming admonishment of his classmates. That day totally perplexed him. Being segregated in the projects for so long, he could not understand why his classmates would not be more accepting of others.

Since that day, he kept in his heart and mind the importance not only of equality but also of being more other-oriented, more understanding, more respectful, and more appreciative of others.

As the oldest son he knew early on that his family was unable to afford any college education for his two brothers and sister. His only option was an apprentice school where he could work and learn the trade of shipbuilding in Newport News, Virginia. Upon completing the four-year program and acquiring a Virginia State Apprenticeship Certificate, he had saved enough money to begin his first entry into higher education. He graduated from the University of Virginia and became a high-school English teacher. He received his first MA in speech communication from Bradley University, a second MA in educational administration and supervision from the University of Tennessee, and his PhD in educational leadership and curriculum from the University of Florida.

He became a speech professor and director of forensics at West Virginia University. Three years later his father-in-law asked him and his wife, Joan, to consider teaching abroad. Off they went, first to teach in Germany. After three years, they were transferred to Holland, in a two-teacher school. After a year's leave to pursue his master's in school administration, they were reassigned to another two-teacher school in England, where they were later transferred to the Cotswold region of England. He was promoted to principal of a K–8 school for five years. He was then promoted to the region-wide language arts coordinator across eight European countries. He became an assistant superintendent in Brussels, Belgium, a superintendent back in the states, and after twenty years with the DoDDS program, he retired and became a dean of the School of Education in Kentucky. Later he accepted an educational leadership professorship in Virginia until his recent retirement.

Even before they arrived in England, they implemented the Validation Program in their own classrooms. They remained dedicated to the weekly program, seeing exceptional changes in their students' treatment of their classmates. Additionally, the students blossomed into positive individuals as the Validation Program defined them as possessing the virtues of quality character.

Over the past thirty-five years, the program has grown enormously across the United States and abroad. Dr. Pirkle has conducted many workshops, training sessions, and presentations at many conferences and forums, the latest of which was in Washington, DC, at the Character Education Partnership (CEP) Forum on November 3, 2012.

From the early days, Dr. Pirkle and his wife, Joan, have supported those educators and others who are committed to helping students develop sound character, giving teachers and others the chance to carry on with the mission. He and his wife are now retired and live in Richmond, Virginia.